A Sailor Called Wet Paint

AND OTHER SECRET STORIES FROM HISTORY

AF673325

Nandini Nayar is the author of over 60 books for children of all ages. Although her postal code says she lives in Hyderabad, in actual fact Nandini inhabits several worlds. Every morning, she sets out on voyages of discoveries and returns with stories about animals and children, trees and seas. It was on one of these journeys that Nandini stumbled across tales about the people in this book. For more information, please visit www.nandininayar.in

A Sailor Called Wet Paint

AND OTHER SECRET STORIES FROM HISTORY

NANDINI NAYAR

Illustrations by Damini Gupta

hachette INDIA

First published in 2023 by Hachette India
(Registered name: Hachette Book Publishing India Pvt. Ltd)
An Hachette UK company
www.hachetteindia.com

SRD

Text copyright © 2023 Nandini Nayar
Illustrations copyright © 2023 Damini Gupta
Photographs: Please see page 147, which may be treated as an extension of the copyright page.
Hand-drawn box used in chapters by Sharanya Kunnath; Other boxes and dividers: by starline, Freepik.com

Nandini Nayar asserts the moral right to be identified as the author of this work.

All rights reserved. No part of the publication may be reproduced, stored in a retrieval system (including but not limited to computers, disks, external drives, electronic or digital devices, e-readers, websites), or transmitted in any form or by any means (including but not limited to cyclostyling, photocopying, docutech or other reprographic reproductions, mechanical, recording, electronic, digital versions) without the prior written permission of the publisher, nor be otherwise circulated in any form of binding or cover other than that in which it is published and without a similar condition being imposed on the subsequent purchaser.

This is a work of creative non-fiction. Names, characters, places and incidents (other than those obviously genuine) are fictitious and any resemblance to real persons, living or dead, or actual events or locales is purely coincidental.

The views and opinions expressed in this book are the author's own and the facts are as reported by her and have been verified to the extent possible. The publishers are not in any way liable for the same. Sources have been referenced and quotes acknowledged to the best of the author's ability. Any inadvertent omissions brought to our attention in writing will be remedied in future editions.

Subsequent edition/reprint specifications may be subject to change, including but not limited to cover or inside finishes, paper, text colour and/or colour sections.

ISBN 978-93-5731-253-0

Hachette Book Publishing India Pvt. Ltd
4th & 5th Floors, Corporate Centre
Plot No. 94, Sector 44, Gurugram – 122003, India

Typeset by Manmohan Kumar, Delhi

Printed and bound in India
by Manipal Technologies Limited

MIX
Paper from responsible sources
FSC™ C043100
FSC www.fsc.org

To all the travellers who left home

CONTENTS

IF YOU'RE WONDERING WHAT THIS BOOK IS *ACTUALLY* ABOUT...

Imagine yourself back in the eighteenth century, walking down a street in London. It is winter and the air is cold. People pull their coats closer and hurry to the warmth of their homes. And then, you hear someone begging, stopping passers-by to say they have no money for food. Further down the street is a woman. Her once-white sari is grimy and she's asking people for help to get home. There's a man sweeping the road and another selling pamphlets at the corner. And they are all from a country thousands of miles away – India. What are all these Indian men and women doing in England? And how did they get here?

We have heard many stories of the Englishmen and women who travelled to India and made it their home. We know that merchants from the English East India

Company first came to India in the seventeenth century. They came as traders, to buy the spices that India had to offer. And they stayed on for over 300 years as colonizers and rulers. In the early days, only Englishmen made the long journey. But around the end of the seventeenth century, women began to travel to India too.

India, with its many languages and cultures diversity, bewildered them. They needed help to make sense of the customs and rules of this new country. Who better than the local people to do this? And so, the English appointed the *bhishti* to carry water into their homes, the *mali* to care for their garden, the *khansamah* to cook for them and the *khitmutgar* to run the household. The people of India followed very strict rules about the kind of work they could and would do. So, the English had to appoint different people to carry out different duties. A small English family often had an entire army of people to serve them. The English could not imagine running their homes without these people. When it was time for them to return to England, they often took some of these helpers with them.

The ships that sailed from England were manned by British crews. But many of these sailors died on the long and challenging journey. Others decided to stay back in India, which promised many opportunities for success. When it was time to return to England, the captains of these ships needed sailors. And so, they hired Indian sailors, who were called lascars.

These were some of the earliest travellers from India to reach the shores of England.

Some of the ayahs spent only a few days in England before they returned to India. A few stayed on with their English families. These women had to get used to the cold weather of England and a lonely life. But these were small discomforts compared to what several other women went through. There are accounts of ayahs who were turned away without being paid or given the return tickets they had been promised.

This was true of the lascars too, who had to wait to find a job on a ship travelling to India. Some captains turned the lascars away without paying them. In other cases, the lascars themselves spent all their money. In both these scenarios, they found themselves in a strange land with no money. Many of these men and women often had to resort to begging on the streets. In many cases, the East India Company sent these poor men and women home.

What were the thoughts of these lascars and ayahs when they reached England? Surely they must have missed home and worried about the family they had left behind. We have no means of knowing because ayahs and lascars were mostly unlettered and have left no accounts of their time in England or of the way they were treated by their English employers.

Fortunately, Englishmen and women, and the captains of various ships have written letters, diaries and stories about their time in India. It is interesting to see how most ayahs and lascars are unnamed in these and are known only by their job titles. It is even more fascinating to learn about the kinds of stories that were commonly accepted about these Indian workers by the English. These tales focused on the laziness of lascars, and their cowardice, while memsahibs were warned about the cunning ayahs who would harm the English baby's health.

When reading accounts written by the English in India, I was struck by all the different ways that the Indians helped ease life for their employers. These men and women displayed enormous courage and loyalty in the way they served their English families. That is why I have made them the heroes of the tales in this collection. All the stories here are based on real people and historical events. All I have done is to dramatize them for the purposes of storytelling.

Writing these stories took me back in time and helped me understand and appreciate the enormous challenges these early travellers faced and the sacrifices they made.

I hope you feel that way too.

THE WOMAN IN THE PAINTING

Let's go back in time, shall we? The English began trading with India in the seventeenth century. They had to rely on their Indian domestic helpers to help them with the everyday aspects of life. While single men managed with a few servants, things changed when they married. In houses with Englishwomen, an ayah was the most important member of the staff. She was the only other woman in the house and acted as the lady's maid. Once a baby was born, the ayah's primary duty was caring for the little one. Although ayahs spoke in their own language with the children, the former also picked up a little English.

'Ayah,' Elizabeth said as soon as she was awake. 'Ayah, where are you?'

'Ayah here,' the ayah replied reassuringly. 'Ayah always here, Missy baba!'

The word 'ayah' comes from the Portuguese word 'aia' and refers to a nursemaid or a nanny - someone who takes care of children. The English rarely bothered to learn the names of the ayahs who worked for them. They were known by the title of Ayah. Sometimes, they were given anglicized names that the English found easy to pronounce.

Actually, many of the memsahibs in India did not have much to do with raising the children. They were left to the care of the ayahs. The children met their parents for just a short while every day. The presence of the ayah allowed the Englishwomen to follow their own interests. Some of them painted, others sketched. Many of them were great travellers and shikaris, and several memsahibs were writers.

Ayah was the centre of Elizabeth's little world. There was Mummy, of course, and there was Papa too. But Elizabeth saw Mummy only in small, hurried snatches. At these times, Mummy called her 'Darling' and hugged her carefully. Mummy didn't know any games. And she didn't like the games Elizabeth wanted to play.

Elizabeth saw Papa in the evening when he came home from work. Papa always picked Elizabeth up and tossed her in the air. Then he set her down and said, 'Run along now, and play!'

Whom could Elizabeth play with?

The English lived in India and benefited from trade with the people here. Their work took them all over the subcontinent. Some Englishmen lived and worked in remote places and others in busy towns. No matter where the English lived, their homes were away from the 'Black Town', as the Indian section was called. The English part of the town had wide roads, with trees and sprawling bungalows with gardens. In large towns, where there were many English families, there were clubs for relaxation and, in the evening, the children played with one another. But what about families that lived in remote places? In such cases, the Indian ayah, *bhishti* and *chowkidar* took the place of playmates for the children.

'Ayah here,' Ayah told Elizabeth. 'Ayah always here.'

Ayah was being literal when she said that she was always there for the children. The house Elizabeth lived in was big and was set in a large compound. Within the compound was Ayah's little house. She only went there to cook and eat. Then she came back, to sleep outside the children's room.

Ayah didn't mind digging in the garden. She found leaves and hard green fruits for Elizabeth to set up a shop. She even pretended to be a customer looking for vegetables at Elizabeth's shop and played her part well. When it was too hot to play in the sun, Ayah took Elizabeth into the cool house and told her stories.

The Indian sun posed the greatest threat to the English. They learnt how to deal with it, wearing sola topis to protect themselves from sunstrokes. Homes were kept cool with woven grass curtains and large *punkhas*, which were moved back and forth by *punkhawallahs*.

Ayah's stories were mostly about gods and goddesses; often, demons too. Sometimes, the tales frightened Elizabeth. She crept closer to Ayah and immediately felt safe. But Sarah, who was much younger, burst into tears. And that woke the baby up, so he began to cry too. The noise of his wails brought Mummy hurrying to ask, 'Ayah, what's the matter?'

At such times, Mummy took Ayah aside and spoke to her. Elizabeth knew she was scolding Ayah. And

The ayah gave English children an introduction to the country of their birth. Ayahs entertained English children with stories from Indian mythology, allowed them to taste sweets from the bazaar and taught them how to light lamps around the house for Diwali.

so, as soon as Mummy went away, Elizabeth ran to hug Ayah. She was hugged back and told, 'Missy baba, be a good girl!'

One day, Mummy came into the room where Sarah and Elizabeth were playing. The baby was asleep in his cradle and Ayah was curled up on the floor close to him. 'Ayah,' Mummy said, 'Ayah, wake up! Quick!'

When Ayah was awake, Mummy said many things to her in clipped, urgent tones. Her words made Ayah tremble and gasp. But she nodded and said, 'Yes, Memsahib, I do it.'

What happened to bring Mummy into the nursery? And what made Ayah tremble? Elizabeth's family lived in the English settlement in Calcutta (now Kolkata). The year was 1756. The Nawab of Bengal, Siraj-ud-daulah, was annoyed that the English were fortifying their settlements. He ordered them to halt and when they refused, he decided to attack them. And now, on 16 June 1756, there were reports of the Nawab's army marching towards the English settlement.

When Mummy hurried away from the room, Elizabeth ran to comfort Ayah. But today Ayah didn't hug her back. Instead, she gently pushed her away and began to pull out clothes from the cupboard. 'Ayah?' Elizabeth was surprised. 'No time now, Missy baba,' Ayah said. 'We must hurry!'

Ayah tied the clothes in a bundle which she then slung on her back, and picked up the baby. 'Missy baba,' she said, 'hold your sister's hand and let us go!'

Where were they all going?

When the news of the Nawab's army marching towards the English settlement came, there was great confusion. Finally, it was decided that the women and children would be moved to Fort William. So that's where the children and Ayah were going.

Sarah didn't want to leave her toys behind. But when she burst into tears, all Ayah said was, 'Hurry!' They rushed out of the house where other servants were dashing about, gathering things into large bundles. Frightened people were milling around the street outside the house. Sarah stopped crying to look around, round-eyed in wonder. Elizabeth saw Mrs Parry, who often visited Mummy, and Mrs Bruton, another friend. But today, no one had the time to stop and talk to the children because they were all scurrying to the fort.

The children walked quickly too, running in spurts to keep up with Ayah. Ayah stopped again and again, to say, 'Hurry now, Eliza baby, Sarah baby!' Near the fort they ran into a large crowd and had to stop.

Elizabeth caught sight of Mummy. Then she was gone, weaving through the crowd, so Elizabeth could no longer see her. Ayah went after her, gently parting people to carve a narrow path. Eliza and Sarah, holding firmly on to her sari, followed her. Then finally, they were past the people and inside the fort. It was cool and damp after the hot summer sun they had just walked in. For a minute, the darkness of the fort filled Elizabeth's eyes, so she could see nothing at all. She stumbled, but Ayah was there, pulling her up before she could hit the rough floor.

Ayah led them into a big room and found a quiet corner. Then, finally, she laid the baby down and sat down, pulling the girls close.

The children, along with other English children and women, spent three days here. Outside, the nawab's soldiers began an attack. The English were unprepared for a battle. They did not have enough men or weapons to fight the nawab's army. In the fort, Ayah played with them and told them stories. When sudden screams and shouts sounded, she hugged them. Elizabeth heard her voice, muffled but comforting: 'Ayah always here.' Elizabeth breathed in the familiar smell of the coconut oil that Ayah rubbed into her hair and was comforted. Ayah didn't leave them for a minute. She fed them and washed them. When the baby cried, she sang him to sleep. But later, it was Ayah who cried. 'Oh, Memsahib,' she wept.

Mrs Cruttenden, the mother of Elizabeth, Sarah and the little baby, had died somewhere in the middle of the bedlam. This was a confusing time for the English and no records state how she died.

And now it was Elizabeth who sang to Ayah, '*Ni baba ni*', patting her on the back with every word. Mummy must have scolded Ayah very badly to make her cry like this. But where was Mummy?

The song that Elizabeth sang was a popular one that ayahs sang to get their charges to sleep. Elizabeth, too young to remember the words, sang her version of it to comfort her ayah. For the English children who spent their early years in India, Indian languages and the Indian way of life were familiar. Years later, they still remembered the warmth of the country and the love they had received from the Indians who had looked after them.

'Missy baba,' Ayah whispered, 'even if Mummy gone, Ayah here. Ayah always here!'

Of course, Elizabeth thought, Ayah was always here. When the loud booms began, Ayah was there, hugging Sarah, Elizabeth and the baby close. Elizabeth felt fear crowd her throat, but Ayah's arms were around her, and the jingle of her bangles in her ears. Elizabeth swallowed her tears and forgot her fears.

Finally, the noise stopped. That was when Papa came, a sad-looking Papa who seemed to have forgotten that he had to toss Elizabeth up in the air. Now, Elizabeth thought, they could go home. But Papa said home was gone and so they were leaving Calcutta, going away from India.

For the Englishmen and women who lived in India, England was home. They were often homesick for it, and talked of the weather and the natural beauty of their own country. By contrast, they found India hot and savage, and waited for the day when they could go home again.

'We are going on a long journey,' Papa said, 'and at the end of that is our new home.' Papa said the grass grew greener there and beautiful flowers danced in the sun. 'And Ayah?' Elizabeth asked anxiously. 'I want Ayah,' Sarah announced.

'Ayah always here,' Ayah told them.

'In the new home too?' Elizabeth wanted to know.

'Always,' Ayah smiled.

Ayah went with them on the big ship that was taking them home. She looked after them during the day, and at night, she slept on the floor of their cabin. There were many other children on the ship, and Elizabeth and Sarah played with them. There were games and parties too.

> Ships going to England always had families with children travelling on them. The ships hired young women who arranged games and activities for them. Most children were accompanied by ayahs who went everywhere with them.

The journey took months and at the end of it was home. But it was not the home Elizabeth had been dreaming of. There was no long veranda there, no garden filled with golden sunlight.

To Elizabeth, born in India, home was always a bungalow with a large veranda. Home was also the people in it, the syce who looked after the horses and the *bhishti* who carried water into the house.

Instead, this was a big house full of strangers. These men and women stared at the children and spoke in funny voices. They didn't understand what the children wanted.

Since children spent most of their time with Indian domestic help, it was the local languages that they learnt first and used the most. It was only when they spoke to their parents that the children used English. Most English children growing up in India only saw their mother and father for a short time each day. And so, the English they spoke was accented. It is easy to see why the English servants could not understand them.

'Oh, Ayah,' Elizabeth called.

'Yes, yes,' Ayah said. 'Ayah here.' She explained to the people in the new home that Elizabeth wanted her *chhota hazri*, or that Sarah wanted to play in the garden.

> *Chhota hazri* referred to the early breakfast that the English ate in India. The English used to wake up early to ride their horses before the day got really hot. They had a cup of tea and some fruit before this, and this small meal was called *chhota hazri*.

The children were glad to have Ayah with them. They clung to her sari and followed the tinkle of her anklets. Ayah never left them, not even when Papa brought an important man to see them. This man, Papa said, was going to paint a picture of the children. The children were dressed in their best clothes and the man spent a lot of time telling them where and how to stand. He pushed them this way and that, asked them to look up and smile. Ayah stayed with them all this time, watching suspiciously to make sure that the children were comfortable. Ayah, the children knew, was always there.

This man was Sir Joshua Reynolds, a well-known portrait painter. Sir Joshua's painting of the children had Ayah in it too. Indian servants were considered a status symbol in England and, therefore, many family paintings included ayahs and helpers.

But one day, Ayah had to go away. She said she was going home, to see her own mummy and papa. 'But you promised,' Sarah wailed.

The English families who brought their servants to England with them did so on the understanding that they would eventually be sent home to India. The children's father kept his word to the woman who had looked after his children, and arranged for her to go back to India.

'You said, *Ayah always here*,' Elizabeth wept.

'Ayah always here,' Ayah said. 'Always with her babies. See!' She pointed to the painting of the three children, with Ayah watching over them. After Ayah went away, Elizabeth often stood in front of the painting, thinking of Ayah.

The children grew older and taller. They got used to the cool grey skies of their new home. But they never forgot the golden sunshine of their other home. People said India was hot, that India was dangerous. They said the children had been caught in the Siege of Calcutta.

'How did you escape unhurt?' they asked.

'Ayah,' said Elizabeth and Sarah. 'Ayah took care of us, Ayah protected us.'

'Ayah?' they were asked. 'Who is that?'

'Her,' Elizabeth said, pointing to the wall, 'the woman in the painting!'

Sir Joshua Reynolds called the painting 'The Children of Edward Holden Cruttenden and Their Ayah' (see next page). It hangs today in the Art Museum of Sao Paulo in Brazil. It depicts the three Cruttenden children with Ayah in the background, watching over them, just like she promised to.

SECRET POST

ABOVE: 'The Children of Edward Holden Cruttenden and Their Ayah'; BELOW LEFT: 'Tysoe Hancock and His Family with an Indian Maid'; BELOW RIGHT: Sir Joshua Reynolds, the painter

2

THE LITTLEST BANGLE

It was the smallest bangle Ruth had ever seen. It was made of silver, with tiny bells hanging on it. It lay on the palm of the Indian ayah, glinting in the morning sun.

Ruth, on her way to school, was held by that dazzling glitter. 'Oh!' she said. 'That's beautiful!'

The Indian woman was sitting on the bench, lost in thoughts as she stared at the bangle. At Ruth's words, she stood up in a hurry and turned around to stare at the young girl. Her eyes were dark and wide with fright. She was draped in white, yards of soft material that fluttered in the morning breeze.

'That,' Ruth pointed to the little circle of silver, 'that's so beautiful!'

The ayah looked down at the bangle and stroked it gently with a finger. When she looked up, Ruth saw that her eyes were full of tears.

'Oh,' she said. 'I am sorry. What can I do?' Even as she asked the question, Ruth knew how silly it was and how useless. All she knew about the woman was that she was Indian. Mama said she worked for the Thornton family in India. And when the family had decided to rent a house in the village of Godalming, in Surrey, they had brought Ayah along.

English families in India had a huge army of servants, each with their own specially defined jobs. As a result, the English were soon used to being served. When it was time to return to England, they took some of these servants back with them.

'She does everything,' Mama said. There was a faint note of envy in her voice. 'She looks after the children all day long. There's a cook too, from India. I hear he makes a good curry.'

Most Englishwomen who lived in England, particularly those from the middle classes, could not afford to employ servants. The lives of their sisters and friends in India appeared like a fairy tale to them, with an army of servants to do everything around the house. It is hardly surprising that they were envious of the lavish lifestyles of the memsahibs in India.

The word 'curry' was used in a very general sense to refer to an Indian dish that required special spices. English families who had spent years in India were used to Indian food and ate it even after they were back in England. Many of these women had recipes for curry powder, which they shared with friends and family. Some Englishwomen even sold curry powder, and soon this dish was a part of the English menu.

But Ruth was not interested in the cook who made good curry. It was the ayah who interested her. Ruth saw her frequently in the mornings. The ayah always looked sad, and often there were tears in her eyes. The littlest bangle was always somewhere on her person, its tiny bells jingling lightly in the silence of the morning. Ruth often stopped to talk to her, ask her how she was. The Indian woman understood very little English, nodding her head to show she was well, and replying in broken English.

Ruth longed to ask about the littlest bangle. It must have come off the wrist of a tiny doll. But where was the doll? And why did memories of the doll make Ayah cry? Mama would be horrified if she knew that Ruth had asked such questions of a complete stranger. Ruth asked them anyway. Ayah listened and then shook her head. 'No unnerstand,' she said. 'No unnerstand.'

'Never mind,' Ruth said, hiding her disappointment behind a wide smile. 'I am sure you'll learn English soon and then you can tell me about that little bangle.' Ayah nodded and smiled through her tears.

The Thorntons spent six months in Godalming. The others in the village soon got used to them and their Indian domestic help. Many of them were even invited over to taste the curry that the Indian cook made.

Ruth became very good friends with Ayah in this time. It was a strange friendship between a young English girl and an Indian woman. Nods and smiles took the place of language as the two talked to each other. Ruth told Ayah about her cat, named May, because she had been found on a warm summer day. In return, Ayah told her about the dogs that lived in her house in India. She yapped and barked most convincingly to explain what she meant. And Ruth, who had never been to India, was immediately able to imagine two small dogs, jumping in excitement. One was called Raja and the other Rani.

There were other words that Ruth picked out of Ayah's speech and began to recognize. One was *ghar*, which Ruth thought meant a building of some kind, from the gestures Ayah made to explain it. Another was *kutta* which Ruth was certain meant dog. Soon, Ruth thought, she would learn other words. Then she would string them together to ask Ayah about the bangle and the doll who wore it.

However, the Thorntons left Godalming before Ruth could do this. They took three carriages full of their trunks, as well as their Indian domestic helpers. For days, Ruth waited for them to return, but they never did. The house was let to another family, and the Thorntons and their Indian retinue soon became a part of village history.

Ruth grew up, and found other things that interested her. When she was 20 years old, she married a man who worked in India.

Ruth bid goodbye to her family and boarded the ship that would take her to her new home. Going to India meant accepting that you were leaving behind your family. Travelling between India and England was expensive and very few young couples could afford this. Ruth would probably not see her family for at least five years.

India was everything people had said it would be – hot and big, crowded and noisy. Ruth fell in love with its golden sunshine and sudden rains. Some Englishwomen, Ruth knew, disliked India. But there

Englishmen who worked in India were discouraged from marrying too early. This was because their salaries were too low to support a family. Ruth's husband had probably spent a dozen years in India by the time she met and married him.

were many who fell in love with the country. Such women were able to enjoy various aspects of Indian life. They travelled around the country, went on shikars and hiked. Many of them developed a keen interest in the flora and fauna of the country.

Ruth hired Indian help and learnt to run a house. The only Indian woman she hired was the ayah.

Ayah was a cheerful woman whose arms were stacked with bangles. The bangles jingled and tinkled when she helped Ruth get dressed. Ayah's lips were stained red with the betel she liked to chew. When a baby was

There were many people to help newly arrived young women in setting up a home in India. The most important of these were the other Englishwomen in the neighbourhood. In addition to this were the books written to help Englishmen and women in India. Books like Flora Annie Steel's *The Complete Indian Housekeeper and Cook*, Maud Diver's *The Englishwoman in India* and Mrs Howard Kingscote's *The English Baby in India and How to Rear It* offered suggestions on how to run a house, how to hire and deal with servants and how to raise babies. Some of them included lists of servants needed, salaries to be paid to them and their duties. Others included recipes and menus for parties.

born to the family, Ayah was ecstatic. She loved the baby and spent hours crooning songs by his cradle. She walked endlessly with the baby on her shoulder, patting him to sleep. She looked at all the gifts that were given to him, and discarded what she didn't like. Only the best, she told Ruth, would do for Baba.

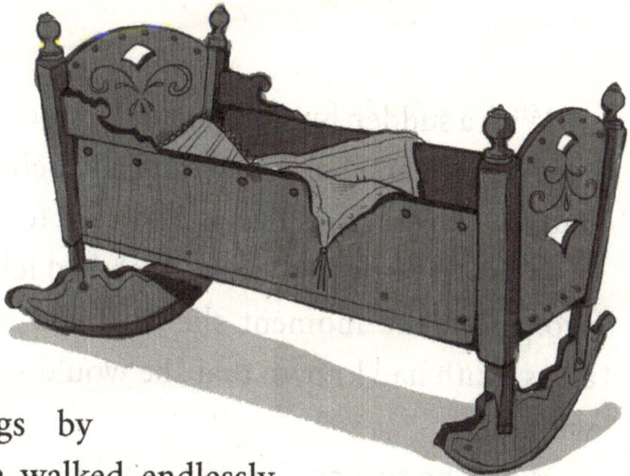

When an Indian family sent a gift for Baba, Ayah was very interested. She watched Ruth pull open the little satin bag and bring out a tiny pair of bangles. Her face split into a large smile. 'Very good, very good,' she told Ruth, nodding happily. 'Good for Baba!'

Ruth looked at the tiny bangle and the little bells hanging on them. But they were not bangles after all. Ayah showed her how they opened so they could be slipped around Baba's ankles. Every time he kicked his feet, they jingled.

Ruth thoughts flew back to the year 1789. That was when she had turned nine, found her cat May and met the crying ayah.

With a sudden lurch, Ruth understood *now*, the reason for Ayah's tears. She had left a baby behind in India and had travelled across the seas to care for someone else's child. Ruth knew now what Ayah had felt all those years ago. From the moment she had held her baby in her arms, Ruth had known that she would soon have to part with him.

When he turned five, she would have to take him to England and leave him there, among strangers, so he could go to school. She would come back to an empty house in India. Perhaps she too would hold his little anklet and remember her child with tears. The thought was too much for her and Ruth burst into tears.

Ayah was surprised and upset. 'Memsahib,' she asked worriedly, 'what wrong?'

Many memsahibs wrote about the pain of parting from their children. Their letters survive, talking of the sorrow of sending children away to England. These women believed that their duty was to stay in India, with their husband. Women who tried to make homes in England for their children were filled with guilt at leaving their husbands alone. But the climate of India and the lack of good schools made it difficult for them to spend time together as a family.

Ruth looked at her baby's ayah. For the first time, she wondered if Ayah had left her own baby behind to care for Ruth's little John.

Ruth wept for all the mothers, in all the corners of the world, parted from their babies and seeking comfort in the littlest bangles in the world.

SECRET POST

An Indian ayah with her English wards

SECRET POST

A typical portrait of an Englishwoman and the ayah, on whom the family depended not just for looking after the children but also for tips on living in India

LEFT: A cookbook by Hannah Glasse, which featured a recipe for Indian curry (BELOW)

To make a Currey *the* India *Way.*

TAKE two Fowls or Rabbits, cut them into ſmall Pieces, and three or four ſmall Onions, peeled and cut very ſmall, thirty Pepper Corns, and a large Spoonful of Rice, brown ſome Coriander Seeds over the Fire in a clean Shovel, and beat them to Powder, take a Tea Spoonful of Salt, and mix all well together with the Meat, put all together into a Sauce-pan or Stew-pan, with a Pint of Water, let it ſtew ſoftly till the Meat is enough, then put in a Piece of Freſh Butter, about as big as a large Walnut, ſhake it well together, and when it is ſmooth and of a fine Thickneſs diſh it up, and ſend it to Table. If the Sauce be too thick, add a little more Water before it is done, and more Salt if it wants it. You are to obſerve the Sauce muſt be pretty thick.

3

THE AYAH'S JEWELS

On 31 December 1849, a ship sailed from Madras (present-day Chennai). The ship was the *Wellesley* and it was bound for London. On board was the usual mix of passengers: English families going home, businessmen on work and soldiers on medical leave. Among these was the family of Dr Darwood, a surgeon with the East India Company. Dr Darwood had been in Madras for 18 years. Now, he was travelling with his wife and their five children. Accompanying them was Ayah Periera, hired to take care of the Darwood children on the long journey.

This was not Ayah Periera's first job. Nor was it the first time she was travelling to England. Caroline Periera had taken up a job working for Sir Edward Barnes in 1824. She had worked for the family for the next several years and when they travelled to England, Ayah went with them. When Ayah Periera finally returned home in 1836, she had managed to save some money from her jobs. Sir Barnes was so pleased with her work that he gave her some land and helped her brother to set up a jewellery business. Ayah Periera was still in contact with the Barnes family. In fact, she planned to meet them when she was in London.

Ayahs entered a family when the children were born. Soon, they became a part of the family, staying on even after the children were sent away to England for their schooling. Grateful employees often gave their ayahs expensive gifts as tokens of their appreciation. Some, like Sir Barnes, gave land to help support the ayahs for the rest of their lives.

Ayah Periera's new employer was nothing like that. And she discovered this when the ship ran into bad weather. The wind pounded the vessel and huge waves splashed on the deck. Water washed into the cabins, drenching everything. Ayah Periera was having a hard time managing the five children. It was at this point that Dr Darwood told her, 'Ayah, I want you to bail out the water from the cabin!'

Ayah Periera stared at him in horror. 'No,' she said. 'I will not do that.'

'I order you to do it,' Dr Darwood shouted.

'And I refuse to do it,' Ayah Periera told him. 'I will fall overboard if I do as you say. I will be of no use to you then!'

Perhaps Dr Darwood saw her logic for he said nothing more. But later, he told her, 'The carpet is all wet, Ayah. I want you to hang it up on the deck! And all the clothes are wet and dirty. Wash them and dry them.'

'No,' Ayah Periera said. 'I have too much to do. I have five children to care for and Mrs Darwood to help. I will not wash the clothes!'

Dr Darwood stared at her in fury. 'You have a long tongue,' he told her. 'You talk too much!'

Ayah Periera said nothing. But from that day, she knew that she and Dr Darwood would never get along.

And so, she was glad when she met Mr and Mrs Smith. They smiled at her and asked how she was. Ayah Periera was happy to have some friends on board. She told them about all the families she had worked for. She showed them her little watch. 'Sir Edward Barnes gave it to me,' she told them.

Mr and Mrs Smith thought the watch was beautiful. They were kind to her and seemed so interested that Ayah Periera shared her big secret with them. She was carrying some money with her and some jewellery too. She had a little pearl necklace, which was a gift for Sir Edward's daughter. 'The other pieces,' she said, 'my brother gave me. I will sell them in London and buy English clothes, knives and forks and fancy things like that. I will sell them in Madras when I return!'

'But, Ayah Periera,' Mrs Smith said, 'you will have to pay duty when we reach London!'

Ayah Periera knew all about customs duty and she was not willing to pay it. 'I will hide my box,' she told the Smiths.

'Don't hide it in the Darwood's cabin,' Mr Smith warned her. 'What if Dr Darwood finds it?'

Where else could Ayah Periera hide her box of valuables then?

'We will hide it for you,' Mrs Smith said. So Ayah Periera placed all her money and jewellery, even the watch that Sir Edward had given her, into a box and handed it to the Smiths. The label on the box said, 'Caroline Periera, Mrs Smith's Ayah'.

'Your box will be safe,' Mrs Smith told Ayah Periera. Ayah Periera watched her new friend put the box away and was relieved. No one would get to her money and jewellery now. Mrs Smith had promised to deliver the box to Sir Edward's house in London. Ayah Periera went back to work, glad that her box would be safe.

The *Wellesley* sailed into London in April 1850, and Dr Darwood disembarked immediately, to look for a place for his family to stay. Ayah Periera finished packing and then went to say goodbye to Mr and Mrs Smith. To her surprise, the steward said they had already got off the ship. Perhaps, Ayah Periera thought, they had been in a hurry. But she was sure they would manage to smuggle her box through the customs, and she would find it when she reached Sir Edward's house.

However, when Ayah Periera finally reached the Barnes's house, there was nothing waiting for her. She knew then that she had been cheated! But Ayah Periera was not going to give up so easily. She found out where the Smiths were living and landed up at their doorstep.

When Mrs Smith saw her, she was shocked. 'How did you find us?' she demanded. 'Who told you we live here?'

Ayah Periera said nothing. She stepped forward and pulled at a watch that Mrs Smith was wearing.

'That was Sir Edward's last gift to me,' she said. 'And I want it back!' But the Smiths refused to return her watch and jewellery. What could Ayah Periera do? The Smiths probably thought that she would go away. But Ayah Periera did something very few ayahs had done. She filed a complaint against them, accusing them of stealing her belongings. And soon, Mr and Mrs Smith were in court, being asked questions by a lawyer.

'Can you explain how you have Ayah Periera's belongings?' they were asked.

'Ayah Periera gave them to us,' Mr and Mrs Smith said. 'In fact, she forced us to take them all! She said we had been good friends to her on the voyage and so she wanted us to have the jewellery and the money.'

> Ayah Periera had the help of Sir Edward's brother in filing this complaint. Often, ayahs and servants who had travelled to England before knew enough about the system to lodge complaints and find solutions to their problems.

This was when Dr Darwood was called, to be questioned about Ayah Periera.

'My wife engaged Ayah Periera,' he told the court. 'And we signed an agreement with her, promising to pay her 300 rupees for working for us. She said she would travel back on her own.'

'What do you have to say about Ayah Periera?' he was asked.

'Ayah Periera is a thief!' Dr Darwood said.

Everyone was shocked. Ayah Periera had filed a complaint and, now, here was Dr Darwood, accusing her of stealing.

'I am not a thief!' Ayah Periera said. 'And Mrs Darwood had nothing worth stealing.'

Dr Darwood filed a separate complaint against Ayah Periera. He said she had stolen a box belonging to his wife.

Now, it was Ayah Periera's turn to be examined and she went to court wondering what she would be asked. But Dr Darwood did not turn up.

Ayah Periera was not the only ayah to have been cheated. The long period of Britain's occupation of India is full of several such stories. Both the East India Company, which was first responsible for Indians in England, and later the British government, let down ayahs and servants. In 1885, a lawyer wrote to the India Office on behalf of his client. The client's ayah was demanding her return passage to India. Would it be illegal, the lawyer wanted to know, for his client not to buy her the return ticket? The India Office assured him that there was no law forcing him to do so, although employers usually did pay for the tickets.

'He is afraid!' Ayah Periera declared.

What could Dr Darwood be afraid of?

'He is afraid because he has not paid me the rest of my salary,' Ayah Periera explained.

Some people laughed to think of a man like Dr Darwood being afraid of a mere ayah. But in the next few days, Dr Darwood arranged for Ayah Periera's return to India. So perhaps Ayah was right.

As for the Smiths, they were declared not guilty. However, there are no records to state why the court decided that they were innocent. And what about Ayah

Caroline Periera's belongings? It seems likely that Ayah Periera did not get her jewellery and money back. It must have been a big loss for a woman in her position. But by going to court against the Smiths, Ayah Periera proved that an ayah was not completely helpless. She proved that if she decided to, an ayah could seek and be granted justice.

Although the law did not seem to have helped Ayah Periera recover her lost property, there were other cases where the law did work. Mrs Eliza Fay had travelled to England in the 1790s and had stopped at St Helena island. While there, she had given away her Indian girl to a Mrs Mason. Mrs Mason was not supposed to sell the girl and had promised to stand by this. But years later, when Mrs Fay stopped again at St. Helena, she was in for an unpleasant surprise. The authorities informed her that Mrs Mason had sold the girl, who was now married and had two children. Mrs Fay was now responsible for sending the woman and her children back to Calcutta! Mrs Fay had to pay 60 pounds!

4

THE MANY 'BABIES' OF AYAH PAREIRA

Neela was dreaming of home. She saw the little hut, with the pumpkin creeper climbing up the side. She saw the way the sunlight filled the little garden, and knew it was mid-morning. The heavy stillness of a summer day lay over the scene. A sound disturbed the silence and Neela frowned in her sleep.

It was a voice, saying something over and over again. She came awake with a little start, and knew at once that home had been a dream. A little pang of sorrow pierced her heart, for home lay behind her now. It would be months, perhaps years, before she saw it again.

For a moment, Neela was overcome with fear at what she had done when she had agreed to accompany Laura baby and Michael baba on the long journey to their home. Neela didn't know where this home was. All she knew was that it lay over the seas, in distant *vilayat*.

'Missy baba,' the voice came again. 'Come to Ayah!'

The ships travelling to England offered first-class and second-class accommodation for the sahibs. But no such arrangements were available for the ayahs and other domestic help travelling with them. They were expected to sleep on the deck of the ship.

Neela recognized the fear in that voice. That was how she felt if Laura or Michael were out of her sight even for a few moments. 'Alice baby, where are you hiding?' the voice sounded desperate.

The attitude of the English to the Indian servants was mixed. On the one hand, they could not manage without them. On the other hand, they did not trust them completely. There were many books written about running homes in India and raising children here. All of them warned the memsahibs not to trust the ayahs completely. Stories circulated about how some ayahs liked to feed the children opium to calm them down.

Neela scrambled to her feet, drew her sari tightly around her and went to look for the owner of the voice. She found her wandering on the deck, where a row of chairs faced the sea. During the day, these were always occupied by people enjoying the brisk sea breeze. They were empty at this time of night.

A worried ayah was shuffling past these. 'What happened?' Neela asked.

The ayah turned at once. 'My baby,' she said, her voice breaking. 'My Alice...I can't find her!'

'I'll help you look for her,' Neela said at once. She had been on the ship only a week but already knew all the places that children liked to play and hide in. She peeped down the stairs and into darkened rooms. 'How did you lose her at night?' she asked.

'I...don't know,' was the reply. 'She just...slipped away from me!'

Neela turned, astonished at an ayah who would let her charge slip away from her. But the ayah's face was in shadow.

'Where were you when she slipped away?' Neela wanted to know. All the ayahs Neela knew always kept their eyes firmly on their children.

> Memsahibs were warned not to trust ayahs and to always keep an eye on them. However, all the accounts written by the English children who grew up in India mention the love their ayahs lavished on them, and their utter dependability in every situation.

'Just here,' the woman said. But she didn't sound very certain, and once again, Neela threw her a curious look. She said nothing, though, as she walked on, scanning the deck for the little girl. A cold wind blew off the sea and Neela shivered, pulling her sari tighter around herself.

'Let's ask the other ayahs for help,' she suggested. Only the gentle sigh of the waves replied.

'Didi,' Neela called. There was no reply. Neela looked around, but there was no sign of the ayah. She could see a group of Indian sailors, the lascars, standing in a knot at the far end of the deck, speaking in low voices. Neela wondered if she should ask them about the missing Alice. Then she decided not to. The ayah had probably found Alice and taken her down to her cabin.

Yawning, Neela went back to the patch of deck that the ayahs had claimed. She lay down and snuggled into her blanket, thinking sleepily of the frantic ayah.

She was woken by the lascars who came with buckets and brushes to wash the deck. Neela went away to get ready for the day. Her night-time adventure was forgotten as she got the children ready. Laura tearfully demanded her horse, which she rode every morning. Neela had a hard time convincing her that her horse would have been very unhappy on the ship. The day passed in the usual routine of walking around the deck, taking the children for their meals and then playing games with them.

Tired from all the exercise, Neela was asleep as soon as she lay down that night.

The ayah's worried voice woke her up and for a moment Neela lay there, cocooned warmly in her blanket, wishing she didn't have to get up. But no one else stirred, so Neela finally struggled to her feet. Still yawning, she set off to look for the ayah. She wondered sleepily what had happened to Alice baby now. But today the ayah turned to ask her, 'Jenny baby and Ron baba... have you seen them?'

'Jenny?'

'They slipped away when I wasn't looking,' Ayah sounded tearful. Neela understood then what was wrong. The ayah was upset. She had seen it happen to other women who had left their own children to care for the Sahib's little ones. These women slept by the baby's cradle, they worried when she was ill, they walked for hours to calm her and get her to sleep. And then, soon after the baba *log* turned five, the sahibs sent them away. They were sent Home, the memsahibs explained, because there were no good schools in India. It was the way of the sahibs and there was nothing anyone could do about it. But the custom did not consider the ayahs who had cared for these children like their own and missed them when they were gone.

The memsahibs were warned against keeping English children in India beyond the age of five. Children did not grow well in India, they were told. The lack of proper schools in India made it necessary for English parents to send the children home. In the nineteenth century, schools for English children were set up in many parts of India, particularly the hills. But children who studied here learnt to speak English with an Indian accent, called 'chee-chee' and so, ambitious English parents continued to send their children back home.

'Jenny?' the ayah pleaded. 'Come to Ayah, Jenny baby.' Neela sighed. How hard it was to ignore this poor woman's sorrow!

Neela was woken up the next night too, and the next. Once Ayah was looking for Susie and another time for her Mark baba. Neela did not mind the disturbed nights. But she did want to talk to Ayah when she was calmer, not searching desperately for the children she had looked after in the past. She had other children in her care now. Why, Neela wanted to ask her, didn't she look after them?

But Ayah was nowhere to be found. She was not among the crowd of ayahs who crept up to the deck after their children were asleep, to spread their bedding and sleep. She was never among the ayahs who gathered to chat about home and the people they had left behind, while the children in their care played the games organized for them. Perhaps, Neela thought, she ate separately. That would explain why she was never to be seen at mealtimes. But someone must have seen her, and so Neela asked the other ayahs.

'Who is she?' they asked. 'What is her name?'

'I don't know,' Neela admitted. 'But she's always looking for her children.'

'Children?' a middle-aged lady asked. 'Why, how many does she have?'

'That's the funny thing,' Neela said. 'Every night she looks for a different child. One night it was Alice, then Jenny, Mark and...'

'It's her,' the middle-aged ayah moaned.

'Her?' Neela echoed. 'Do you know her then? Who is she?'

'Ayah Pareira!' several voices answered.

Everyone, it seemed, knew Ayah Pareira.

'She's made many trips across the seas,' one ayah told Neela.

'She took care of different children on each trip,' another woman explained.

'And how many trips did she make?' Neela asked.

'One hundred!'

'I heard it was eighty-six.'

'No, no, she made 75 trips!'

'Fifty-four trips,' Ayah Minnie said. The clamour of voices died down as she continued. 'That's how many times she travelled with different children, making sure they ate properly, and caring for them when they were sick,' Ayah Minnie sighed.

'Fifty-four trips,' Neela said, awed. This was her first trip and already she was longing to be off this ship, longing for the familiar world of home. How had Ayah Pareira done it?

The English children who were sent away from India always remembered the warmth and the love of the people who had looked after them in their childhood, particularly their ayahs. The letters they sent to their parents in India had memories of the past and remembrances to the ayahs. For the ayahs too, life changed when the children in their care were sent away. While many of them took up other jobs, they never forgot the children.

'It was not easy,' Ayah Minnie said. 'She told me it was like losing a bit of herself, each time she said goodbye to her *bachchas*!' The other ayahs nodded, because they knew how that felt.

'And what does she do now?' Neela wanted to know.

Ayah Minnie stared at her.

'I mean,' Neela said, 'is she still escorting children? She must be on her fifty-fifth trip now!'

'She's dead!' Ayah Minnie said.

'What?' Neela echoed. 'Dead?' Then, as realization struck here, she stammered, 'Then...what did I...see?'

'You saw Ayah Pareira,' Ayah Minnie said. 'And she was doing the one thing that she loved doing – being an ayah to her children!'

Mrs Antony Pareira was an ayah who was believed to have made 54 trips to England, taking care of different children on each journey in the early twentieth century. However, recent researchers have questioned if it was possible for one woman to have made so many journeys. The lack of any records makes it difficult to prove things either way and we must assume that even if Ayah Pareira didn't make exactly that many trips, she made enough of them to become a legend!

That was not the last time Neela was woken up by that anxious voice. Every time she heard it, she left the warmth of her blankets to help Ayah Pareira look for the children in her care. The ship never ceased moving, cutting through the dark seas, taking Neela closer and closer to the day when she too would have to say goodbye to the children whom she cared for.

5

WHICH WAY IS HOME?

The early merchant ships that sailed to India in the 1600s carried only men. It was only towards the end of the seventeenth century that Englishwomen began to travel to India. Those who came with children often brought nannies with them. But these English nannies were expensive. Besides, they knew nothing of India and often complained about the living conditions. Some of these women went back to England, while others left their jobs to marry and settle in India. The memsahibs soon realized that not only did Indian women take better care of the children, but they could also be paid less.

The year was 1908. Trains arrived huffing and puffing loudly at London's King's Cross Station. Doors clanked open and people stepped on to the platform. The air filled with the chatter and movement of passengers arriving from different places.

People stood for a moment, looking around the huge railway station, and then, picking up their bags, they set off. They made their way to the doors that led out. They stepped through these and were swallowed up by the city crowds.

A few of them, however, paused to look curiously at a group standing to one side. There was nothing unusual about the family of four – the well-dressed parents and their two children. The husband and wife huddled together, speaking urgently. The fifth member of the party stood a little apart. In fact, at first glance, she appeared not to belong to the group. But the children occasionally spoke to her, to which she responded with nods and smiles.

She was an Indian woman dressed in white. A red band ran around the edge of her clothes. She stood patiently, her eyes fixed on a distant point. Any small movement

Ayahs usually wore white saris, sometimes with a red border. Earrings, bangles, nose- and toe-rings were the jewellery they often wore. Most ayahs were illiterate, with very little knowledge of the world. This meant that they often travelled to England without the warm clothes needed there, and suffered from the cold.

she made set off a musical jingling of the bangles on her wrists. Heavy earrings dangled from her ears and silver rings flashed on her toes. Passers-by, hurrying past with their luggage, wondered why she was not dressed in warm clothes. Surely she must be cold!

Yes, she was cold. But she had worked as an ayah for years now and her experience had taught her to say as little as possible. Memsahibs didn't like being told things. Particularly in front of the sahibs. She had also learnt that most memsahibs were kind and remembered to ask if she was hungry or if she needed anything. The last memsahib she had worked for had been like that. She had engaged Ayah in Bombay (now Mumbai), to travel with her to England. There had been two small children to care for on the long voyage. Ayah

Travelling to England was a big challenge for any Indian worker. The journey was long and often dangerous. This meant that they had no idea how long it would take, and when they would finally be back. It also meant surviving in an alien country without the support of friends and family. For many Indians, travelling across the seas meant that they would lose their caste. They were forced to go through a purification ceremony once they returned home.

had worked for many memsahibs, but all the jobs had been in different parts of India. She had thought long and hard about leaving her country for this new job.

Finally, she had accepted it because she needed the money. And because Memsahib had promised to send her home as soon as possible. 'I will arrange your passage home, Ayah,' Memsahib had told her. And Memsahib had kept her word. As soon as they were in London, she had begun to look for someone who was going out to India. 'We need to find you a good family,' she had told Ayah. 'Someone who will take care of you.'

The English families that engaged Indian women to go to England with them paid for their passage. In addition to this, the women were paid a salary. This was often the temptation for Indian women to leave their homes and families behind and go to England.

Some English families paid for their ayahs to go back home. Those who wished to save the expense of paying for the ayah's return journey, arranged another job for her. This meant that the new employers would take care of the passage and other expenses.

That was why Memsahib was happy when she finally found Mrs Drummond. The Drummonds were going to

Why did the Drummonds engage Ayah?

Till 1857, it was the East India Company that operated in India. After the uprising in 1857, this changed. From 1858, India became a part of the British Empire and was now controlled by the government. The government appointed the officers who travelled to India in large numbers, bringing their families with them. Most families travelled with someone who would help out on the long voyage. This was particularly true of families with children. Many women preferred to hire an Indian ayah to travel to India with them. This is probably the reason Mrs Drummond hired Ayah.

She must have hoped to use Ayah as an interpreter once they were in India. Ayah could also help her set up home and find her way in the new country.

India and wanted an ayah for their children. And so, they had engaged Ayah.

First, though, they had spent two weeks in Scotland. Ayah had gone with them and found Scotland cold and damp. She had been glad to leave and travel by train to London. Mrs Drummond had told her that they would board the ship that would take them to India. The thought of going home filled Ayah's heart with gladness.

Mrs Drummond said the ship would take them to Bombay port. From there, Ayah would have to find her own means of going home. Home lay beyond the busy streets of Bombay, a long way by bullock cart. But at the end of the dusty journey were her little Raja and Ratan. Raja had been a baby when she had left home. He must be much older now. Ayah was filled with a sudden fear. Would her baby know her? Ayah pushed the thought away and thought instead of what she would do with the money Drummond Memsahib would give her at the end of the voyage.

The ayahs who cared for English children and made the lives of their memsahibs so much easier, did so at the cost of their own families. They left behind their children and families to care for the English children because they needed the money they earned.

Ayah sighed gently and looked at Sahib and Memsahib. They had stood there for so long, talking and talking. But now she saw that they had finished. The Sahib picked up the bags and said something to the children. The children nodded, threw her a quick look and then followed their father. Wait, Ayah wanted to call out, I will care for the children. That's my job. That's why you hired me. She took a hasty step forward. That was when Memsahib said, 'Wait, Ayah Mary.'

That was not Ayah's name but she said nothing. Memsahibs liked to name their ayahs and they always picked names they liked, names that were familiar and easy to remember. She had been Betty on her journey from Bombay. She didn't mind being Mary on the way back.

Memsahib said something but it was difficult to understand in the noise of the station. Ayah waited for her to explain. Instead, Memsahib handed her some money and walked away.

'Memsahib,' Ayah called. But her voice was lost in the loud clatter of King's Cross Station. Ayah watched Memsahib walk away. Soon, she was lost in the bustling, jostling crowd. Ayah waited for her memsahib to return so she could ask her about the money. She was supposed

Ayahs who travelled to England did not usually have a passport of their own. Instead, their names were included on the passport of the memsahibs. The passports listed the name that her memsahib had chosen for the ayah. The most common of these were Mary and Flora. In many cases, the ayah was simply called by the name of the family she worked for. In this case, Ayah would have been Ayah Drummond.

to pay Ayah at the end of the journey, when they were finally in Bombay. Then why had Memsahib given her money now? Was it because she was pleased with Ayah?

Ayah stood there for hours, waiting for her memsahib and the children. People came and left on trains. New trains arrived, and passengers surged out of the compartments and hurried away to the warmth and comfort of their homes.

Ayah could feel fear beating an urgent tattoo in her chest. After all, she was in a new place where she knew no one. And yet she waited for her family to come back. Hours passed before she accepted what she had feared – Memsahib Drummond had abandoned her, left her at the busy King's Cross Station like a piece of luggage forgotten by a rushing passenger. Ayah's eyes filled with tears, but she blinked them away and swallowed the hard

Mrs Drummond's ayah was not the first woman to be abandoned by her employers! The people of England got used to seeing these homeless women wandering around, begging. The British government decided that the East India Company had to bear the cost of sending these Indians home. This would mean a lot of expenditure for the Company. And so, from the 1770s, the Company came up with a new rule. Anyone who wanted to take an Indian to England had to deposit some money with the Company. In the beginning, this amount was 50 pounds. Later this was raised to 100 pounds. However, this system only lasted up to 1844. After this, English families continued to take Indian servants to England. If they had no further use for them once they reached England, they abandoned them without any fear of being punished or fined.

lump in her throat. Then she moved away from the spot she had stood in for hours just so that the Drummonds could find her when they came back.

Then, she stepped forward and stopped a man hurrying towards the exit. 'Home,' she said. 'Which way...home?'

Who was this ayah? Where did she come from and what was her name?

These are details that have been lost to us. All we know is that Mrs Drummond hired her to accompany

What were Ayah's thoughts when she realized that she had been abandoned in a strange place? Unfortunately, there are no records written by ayahs. This is because usually ayahs could not read and write. Also, because their jobs kept them too busy to record their experiences. And so, we can only imagine what her feelings were on this occasion.

the family on their voyage to India. But when they reached King's Cross Station, the Drummonds changed their minds. They handed the ayah one pound and went away. The ayah found her way to Thomas Cook, where she had been hired by Mrs Drummond. From there, she was sent to the Ayahs' Home.

Did she finally go home? There are no records to show that she did. But the Ayahs' Home was very efficient

Not all English employers were as lucky as Mrs Drummond. In June 1819, there is an account of a woman brought from India by one Mr Scott. After a quarrel with Mr Scott, this woman sought help from the East India Company. The Company was convinced by her case and forced Mr Scott to pay for her stay in England and her ticket home.

when it came to finding jobs for ayahs who wished to return home. So, we must hope that she did indeed find her way home. And what of Mrs Drummond? Like many others who abandoned the Indian women who came to England to work for them, Mrs Drummond too escaped punishment for her cruel, heartless treatment of the ayah.

A HOME FOR AYAHS

While some ayahs were able to appeal to the East India Company who funded their way home, others were not so lucky. Where did these women go? It was only around 1855 that the people of England woke up to the plight of these homeless women. They were found in cheap lodging-houses in the poor sections of London. The women were forced to pay high rents for the dirty and overcrowded rooms. When their money ran out, they were thrown out and had to rely on begging.

Around the 1890s, an Ayahs' Home was set up in London. Ayahs from India and 'amahs' from China lived here, along with nannies from other places, The Home not only provided a safe place for the women, but also helped them find a job that would help them travel home.

IN THE AYAHS' HOME (HACKNEY).

6

WHAT CAN A LASCAR DO?

The East India Company ships that sailed to India from 1608 were manned by an English crew. But the long journey and the heat of the tropics caused many deaths among the English sailors. When it was time for the ships to return to England, the captains found that they were short of crew. As a result, they employed Indian sailors for the return journey. These sailors were called lascars.

Although the Navigation Act of 1600 stated that 75 per cent of the sailors on a British registered ship had to be English, lascars continued to be employed. However, British crew members rarely appreciated the lascars or found anything good to say about them. Often, these uneducated men were cheated of the money that was owed to them and left to manage on their own, with no means, in an alien country.

Many ships lay in the port of Surat. Some of these had just arrived and groups of coolies were unloading them. Other ships were preparing for a new voyage. Among these was the *St. George,* which had spent the last few months in the port. Now, in early 1667, the ship was ready to sail home to England.

The ship bustled with activity. Sacks of spices were being carried into its hold. Then came the bales of fine soft cotton and glittering lengths of silk. In another part of the vesssel fresh vegetables, sugar, salt, tea, rice, flour, ghee and oil were being loaded.

Why was the ship carrying items like vegetables and oil? This was because the journey to England was a long one. It usually took six months, but sometimes the ship ran into storms, and this caused delays. That's why the vessel had to carry enough food to last the people on board.

The tank of fresh water was full and had been inspected by Captain Lord himself. The captain walked about the deck, shouting orders at the men. 'The *ghat serang*...where is he?' he asked his officer. 'He promised to bring some men today!' But the officer didn't know where the *ghat serang* was or when he would come with the lascars.

'Lascars,' Captain Lord muttered angrily, 'what can they do?'

The general belief among the European captains was that lascars were not as capable as European sailors.

The word 'lascar' came from *khalasi* or *lashkar*. Indian men who wanted to work as sailors sometimes signed up with ships. But the more popular way was for groups of sailors to be employed. The men who belonged to such groups were called lascars.

How did the captain of a ship find a group of lascars? The captain used an agent or a contractor who supplied lascars. This agent was called *ghat serang*. The *ghat serang* helped lascars by providing them a place to stay and giving them an advance on their salaries. In return, he collected a part of the lascars' salaries as his commission. A *ghat serang* himself did not sail on the ship.

Captains said they were useless in any kind of emergency. And yet, Captain Lord needed them to sail his ship back to England. The wind was picking up. Soon, the captain knew, it would be time to sail.

But how could he set sail without more sailors?

'Sahib,' someone said behind him. The captain swung around and found himself facing an Indian man. It was the *ghat serang* he had been waiting for. 'I am Mangoo,' the man introduced himself.

'And your men?' Captain Lord demanded.

'Here,' Serang Mangoo waved his hand. A group of men appeared.

This was the 'age of sail'. This meant that ships were powered by the wind. There was no time fixed for the ship's departure because ships had to set sail when the wind was in the right direction. Things changed when steam-powered ships began to operate on sea routes, in the 'age of steam'.

'Hmm,' Captain Lord said, looking carefully at them. He would need, he decided, at least eight men. When the men had been chosen, there was the question of a *serang*. A *serang* was the head of the lascar crew. He carried their problems to the captain and conveyed the captain's orders to the lascars. A *tindal* was the headman. He oversaw a group of men, and big ships sometimes had more than one *tindal*. That done, Serang Mangoo waved the other men away.

'Now,' he smiled at the captain, 'we discuss the pay!' It was a long discussion, and at the end of it the captain handed over some money to Serang Mangoo. This was an advance on the lascars' pay. The rest of the money would be handed over to them at the end of the voyage.

The *St. George* set out the next day. The journey would be a long one and the *St. George* would take anywhere between seven to nine months to reach England. On some days, the sea was as still and smooth as a mirror. On other days, brisk winds filled the sail and sent the ship racing over the waves. Storms swept out on the open sea, battering the ship with heavy winds and fierce sprays of water.

Through all this, the lascars went about their work, singing songs and chatting. When it was time to eat, their cook brought along a pot of rice and some curry. The lascars gathered in a circle around the pot and settled down on the deck to eat. They chattered to each other in their own languages and the captain shook his head at how little they knew. Why, they spoke no English. The captain had to speak to Serang Sahoo when he wanted anything done. Serang Sahoo himself only knew enough to say, 'Yes, sir, Kaptaan Sahib!' Not enough, Captain Lord thought, to be of any real use.

The lascars did not eat with the European sailors. The food they ate was also different. Ships that travelled with lascars carried rice, dal, salted fish, tamarind, ghee and spices. This food was prepared by the lascars' cook. The lascars liked to eat it on the deck, sitting together.

He discovered soon how very wrong he was when the *St. George* finally docked in London. Winter had set in and, in their thin clothes, the lascars were sure to feel the pinch of the sharp wind. But nothing could dampen their spirits now that the voyage was finally at an end. They laughed

and talked as they planned how they would spend their pay. No one noticed the captain talking to two of the lascars. And no one saw the captain walk off the ship with Shankar and Dinoo, the two lascars.

After months at sea, the lascars were eager to enjoy all the things that they had missed. Often, they ended up spending all their money on drinking and gambling. This left them penniless in a foreign land, where they knew no one.

Several hours passed before Captain Lord came back to the ship. He was humming lightly to himself, and a small smile played around his lips. It was easy to see that he was pleased about something. But the smile was wiped off his face when he walked back on the ship.

The lascars were all there, squatting on the ground. They seemed to have sat there for hours. Serang Sahoo, a lean man with a worried face, sprang to his feet when he saw the captain.

'Where are they?' he demanded. 'Dinoo and Shankar – where are they?' The *tindal,* a middle-aged man with a thick moustache, stood close to the *serang,* nodding his head.

'Sold them,' Captain Lord told them. 'I sold your precious lascars!'

A wail burst from Serang Sahoo. Then, with a shriek of rage, he leapt at the captain. In a minute, the other lascars joined him. The officers, seeing their captain being attacked, rushed to help. Finally, they managed to get Serang Sahoo off Captain Lord.

'Your lascars,' Captain Lord panted, 'get them off my ship and go!'

'But you have not paid us,' Serang Sahoo reminded him.

Captain Lord only said, 'Off my ship!'

The lascars, once they understood what was happening, protested in loud voices. But the other officers of the ship paid no attention to their protests and simply pushed them off.

Then Captain Lord told them, 'You will not get a penny out of me!'

'But, Captain,' the First Mate asked, 'what if they make trouble for us?'

Captain Lord looked down at the lascars standing in a little huddle on the dock. 'Those lascars and their *serang*?' he demanded. 'Why, they don't speak a word of English. What can a lascar do?'

Captain Lord was not the only captain to think that lascars could do nothing to fight back. The lascars were often beaten and starved on ships. Once they reached the destination, they had to wait for weeks for their salary. Some unscrupulous captains refused to pay them. Since the lascars did not speak the language and knew no one in England, they often had to resort to begging on the streets. While this annoyed many citizens of England, there were others who felt sorry for the lascars. Charitable organizations sprang up in London to help the lascars with free food and clothes.

The captain turned and walked away to supervise the unloading of the ship. Captain Lord thought no more of the lascars he had turned away without their pay. Perhaps he would not have been so calm had he known of their rage at what had happened. Or the determination of Serang Sahoo and the *tindal* to get the money owed to them. After much thought, the *serang* and *tindal* lodged a complaint against Captain Lord with the directors of the East India Company.

The directors set up a committee to find out what had happened on the *St. George*. The committee asked questions and submitted a report to the directors. The report showed that the *serang* and *tindal* had been speaking the truth. Captain Lord had not paid the lascars their salary. What was more, he had sold two lascars to Captain Tilman! They were even now on their way to America on the ship *Constant Friendship*. The committee acted immediately. They sent an urgent message to the Royal Collector of Customs. This was where the ship would get the final clearance before leaving for America.

Serang Sahoo and the *tindal* showed remarkable courage in appealing to the directors of the East India

The *serangs*, remember, were responsible for the lascars in their team. The lascars came from different parts of India and were usually strangers to one another when they set out on the voyage. However, their experiences on the ship brought them together and forged strong bonds among them. They not only helped each other, but they also often fought on behalf of their friends. In this case, the *serang* and *tindal* decided to fight for their rights by appealing to the directors of the East India Company. The Company was held responsible for the ships that plied between England and India. This included citizens of India who happened to be in England.

Company. They were not the first to do so, and they were certainly not the last. Some *serangs* who felt that the directors of the Company would not be able to help them, sought help from royalty. The *serangs* of the ships the *Mermaid* and the *St. George* (yes, again) appealed to Queen Anne in 1713.

Captain Tilman had completed all formalities before he set out for America. And so, he was surprised when his ship was stopped by the Royal Collector of Customs and the captain was asked to return the two lascars he had bought from Captain Lord. This, Captain Tilman refused to do. He had paid a lot of money for these lascars. The East India Company had to pay him for the two lascars.

Dinoo and Shankar were overjoyed to find that they were going back to London. Soon, they were with their friends. The East India Company arranged a place for all the lascars to stay till they could be sent home to India.

The East India Company bought clothes and food for the lascars and found a place for them to stay. Then, a few months later, the Company sent them all home to Surat on the ship *Return*.

As for Captain Lord, he had to pay all these expenses to the Company. He understood then just what lascars, *serangs* and *tindals* could do!

THE EAST INDIAMEN

As the name suggests, the East Indiamen ships were big sailing ships that were typically built between the sixteenth and the nineteenth centuries by European countries for trade with southern Asia. The Portuguese and Dutch sailors and traders were the first to use these. Other countries such as Denmark, France, Sweden and England also used these ships. The English eventually became the leaders in trade. In 1600, Elizabeth I, the queen of England, granted the East India Company the sole right to trade between the Cape of Good Hope and Cape Horn. This was limited later and taken away in 1834.

English East Indiamen usually sailed between England, the Cape of Good Hope and India, stopping mainly at Bombay, Madras and Calcutta. They often went on to China.

7

THE KIDNAPPING OF THE LASCARS

The year was 1798. The past winter had been very severe but now, finally, it showed signs of going away. The sun was mild, but Ghasee Ram enjoyed the gentle warmth of its rays. He was sitting on the steps that led down to the river, not really thinking about anything, when he heard a sound. It was a piercing sound, a 'pssst' that cut through the shouts of the fish sellers, the distant beat of a drum and the shrieks of children playing. He looked around but saw no one nearby. An empty boat bobbed gently on the water.

'Psst!' The sound came again, and Ghasee Ram's heart began to beat faster.

'Beware the evil that hides to strike,' his grandmother always said. Ghasee Ram hurriedly got to his feet, eager to get away from this hidden danger. At that moment, a man sat up in the boat.

'Where are you going?' he demanded and Ghasee Ram jumped at his voice. 'Don't you want to work?'

Ghasee Ram had been ready to run away. At these words he stopped and turned back. 'Yes,' he said eagerly. 'What's the job?'

'The captain of that ship is looking for some men to load it,' the man said. He was pointing to a ship that lay some distance away.

'But…that's a *firangi* ship,' Ghasee Ram said nervously.

Ghasee Ram had reason to be nervous. Although English ships had been sailing to India for the past several years, the relations between Indian lascars and the English captains were not good. There were constant complaints from the lascars about not being paid enough or on time. The English disliked having to deal with the *ghat serangs* and tried hard to get rid of them.

'It's only a loading job,' the man said. 'Half a day's work and you will have your money in your hands.'

The thought of earning money tempted Ghasee Ram. And yet he hesitated. 'There are others,' the man told him, 'who want to earn money. They are sure to jump at an opportunity like this. So…'

'I'll do it,' Ghasee Ram blurted out. He tried not to think of his grandmother's warning as he got into the little boat. Instead, he thought of how good it would be

In 1793, the Bengal government appointed a Marine Register Office where the lascars would have to register themselves. The wages were fixed too. However, the English were horrified to realize that their plan failed because the *ghat serangs* prevented sailors from signing up. In a short time, the English were asking for a return to the old system.

to earn some money. Perhaps he could buy some fresh fish with it. Even as Ghasee Ram was daydreaming about this, the other man was rowing towards the ship. It grew larger and larger, filling Ghasee Ram's eyes.

Be careful, he told himself, stay alert. But when he finally got on the ship, he found there was nothing to worry about. Instead, there was a group of sailors standing in a little knot, discussing something. They all looked around to stare at him, and Ghasee Ram saw a few familiar faces among them. There was the man who lived three doors away from Ghasee Ram's house. Ghasee Ram didn't know his name, but it was reassuring to see a face he knew. There was another man Ghasee Ram remembered seeing in the temple. There were two young brothers who always won the wrestling matches. Ghasee Ram, as a spectator among a shouting, cheering crowd of men, remembered watching them fight.

A little rush of gladness filled him at the sight of all the known faces. He felt suddenly courageous and hopeful, and set to work with a will. He hefted a sack on his back and walked to the hold. By the time all the sacks had been dropped into the hold, all his fears were forgotten. Laughing at something one of his new friends had said, Ghasee Ram jumped into the hold. It was darker here, but enough light came in through the square hole for them to see where they had to arrange the sacks. The men set to work, passing the sacks along a line. Dimly, Ghasee Ram noticed that the ship was dancing on the waves.

'The water is getting rough,' someone said. Badru, who was a friend of Ghasee Ram's friend, said, 'I sneezed three times this morning. Whenever I do that, a storm strikes!' There were shouts of laughter at this, and Badru was replying to them when the ship heaved hugely.

There was a cry of alarm and all laughter died down. In the silence, Badru's voice was very loud. 'See?' he said smugly. 'Three sneezes and…' The ship heaved violently at that moment and Badru broke off. 'Something's not right,' he said. 'I am going to look.'

He clambered up the ladder and disappeared from view. The waiting men heard his feet pound on the deck. Then, they heard the returning thumps of his feet. His face appeared in the open square above them.

'The ship…it has set sail!' Badru shouted.

There was a mad scramble for the ladder. Pushing, shoving and cursing, they erupted out of the hold and stood staring. Over the sides of the ship, they could see the waves moving past and knew that Badru had been right – the ship had pulled up anchor and was moving along the water. Already the shore was a distant line with fuzzy-leaved trees and roofs that ran into each other.

'Turn around,' someone shouted. 'We want to go home.'

The others took up the shout and for a few moments the ship resounded with cries of, 'We want to go home!'

'The ship cannot turn around,' someone said behind them. They whirled around and saw the captain there, watching them. Behind him stood a knot of English sailors.

'But we want to go home,' they shouted.

'You can swim ashore,' one of the English sailors suggested. There was a little burst of laughter.

Only Ghasee Ram stood staring at the jumble of houses getting smaller and smaller by the minute. His house was too far away to get a last glimpse before they

The captain made this suggestion because he knew that the men could not jump overboard. Strangely enough, the lascars, who spent most of their lives on the water, could not swim. This was one of the reasons for several lascar deaths during voyages.

sailed away. The English captain had tricked them. And now, they were setting out on a long journey.

What happened to the sailors? Captains rarely mentioned lascars in the records they maintained. So, it was difficult to get information about the sailors on the ship. Some of the lascars must have died on the long

Surely, the captain of a ship did not really kidnap the lascars? Yes, he did. The ship must have sailed from England, losing European sailors to the heat on the way. A few other sailors must have deserted and disappeared in the vast crowds of India. How could the captain get his ship back to England? He knew very well that hiring lascars meant engaging with *ghat serangs*, which he didn't want to do. And that's why he trapped unsuspecting villagers into getting on the ship and sailed away.

and challenging voyage. Once they reached England, the captain must have simply let the lascars off his ship, with not a thought about how they would get back home.

The laws of the time would have made it difficult for these lascars to get home. The ships sailing from England could appoint only a few non-English crew members. This meant that the lascars would have to wait for a long time before they found a job on a ship sailing to India. While they waited, they would have to pay for rent and food in London. It was very likely that their money would run out, leaving them homeless and starving.

Was the captain of the ship punished for kidnapping the lascars? There are no records of what happened to the captain or to the kidnapped lascars. However, after this incident, lascars in India refused to work on ships bound for England. The governor general himself assured them that the captain would be punished and that nothing like this would happen again. But the lascars remained suspicious and continued to boycott foreign ships.

A SAILOR CALLED WET PAINT

13 March 1800
This is the diary of Rachel Babbington, aged 13 years and eight months (*almost* a young lady!). On 10 March, we sailed from Calcutta on the *Rosa Maria*. The captain (I shall call him that even though he's my father) says

The journey from India to England was a long one, with very little entertainment for the passengers. Many of them kept diaries or wrote letters during the journey where they mentioned the regular routine and also special events. Writing these journals helped to pass the time and to share sailing experiences with family members. Such accounts invariably mentioned the lascars and it is from these that historians have pieced together information about conditions at sea, and particularly the situation of the lascars.

the winds are favourable and the weather perfect for a voyage to England.

The captain says there is enough food on board to last us for the journey. Walking on the deck, you can hear the clucking of hens and the cries of the other animals. The tank of fresh water too has been filled. But Mama has her own cans of fresh water in our cabin.

In the early days of travel, ships offered passengers only a bare cabin. The passengers were expected to furnish it for the voyage. Experienced travellers also carried some food with them and their own stock of fresh water. Drinking water on the ship was rationed out and towards the end of the journey, it often smelt unpleasant. Food too often spoilt during the many months at sea.

The rice and dal and spices for the Indian sailors have been carried on board too. The captain says they are called lascars. They have a *tindal* who manages them and a *serang* who is in charge of them. The captain says the *serang* has a difficult time controlling the lascars. The lascars don't look like troublemakers to me. It must be the *serang* who doesn't know how to control them.

All ships with lascars on them had to carry separate food for them. The East India Company had strict rules about the nature and quantity of food to be given to the lascars employed on their ships. Lascars were cheaper to feed than European sailors, the food for the former costing only half the amount spent on feeding the European crew. Sailors who did not follow rules on the ship were punished by having their food rations stopped. In the case of the lascars, this meant that they were given only rice and water.

17 March
We have now left the noise and crowds of Calcutta behind, and are sailing on the open sea.

18 March
The captain says the weather is good. If it keeps up like this, we should be home sooner than planned. Mama says this is because Papa is a good captain. But I think it is because of the lascars. Papa snorted when I said this. Lascars, he says, are no good. It is the European sailors who do all the work. One European, he says, does the work of three lascars.

It was a commonly held belief among the Europeans that lascars did less work than European sailors. This allowed the Europeans to pay the lascars much less than what they paid the European sailors. They said lascars could not work in the cold season because they came from a hot country. This was part of the narrative that grew around lascars. Another one, that began in the age of steam, was that lascars were best suited to work in the engine rooms because they came from hot countries. Despite this, the demand for lascars never went down. In fact, many ship captains preferred lascars because they were easier to handle and more likely to follow orders.

That can't be right. Every time I look, the lascars are hard at work. They are awake long before us to scrub the deck and then wash it clean. Their *serang* blows a whistle to order them around and I hear it blow all day long, from different parts of the *Rosa Maria*.

After the decks are cleaned, the lascars polish the brass. Then, they are sent all over the ship, to repair and polish. A ship needs a lot of looking after, and I think the lascars do most of the jobs that need doing. They don't complain, either. Instead, they sing all the time. The captain says this is because they have just got an advance on their pay. But some of their songs sound sad. So, they can't really be happy all the time, can they?

Ship captains handed over an advance on the lascars' salary to the *ghat serang* before the ship set sail. But very little of it actually went to the lascars. The *ghat serang* took his commission out of this advance. Most lascars had to borrow money from the *ghat serang* and now, this had to be paid back. Once this was done, the lascars were left with very little money.

29 April

We have had some rough days. The captain says the storms and the strong wind are normal for this time of year, but there was nothing normal about my stomach. It heaved with the movement of the sea, and it made me very ill. The captain said it was going to be a smooth run now. We have rounded Galle Point and are in the Indian Ocean.

Everyone cheered up when they heard this. It made home seem a little closer. The lascars didn't look very happy. I wondered why. Then I realized that our homes were in different parts of the world. Every mile we travel takes us closer to our homes and them, further away from theirs.

A lascar who took up work on a ship travelling to England had no means of knowing when he would return home. The voyage took anywhere from six to nine months and the sailors often encountered storms. The cold weather and the bad diet caused many lascars to fall ill. Once in England, lascars often spent months waiting to find a job on a ship returning home. This was because the rules of the time stated that 75 per cent of the sailors on the ships sailing from England had to be British. So, a sailor could end up spending a few years away from home.

3 May

The songs of the lascars are back, and I am glad.

The accounts written by the passengers on ships mention the songs sung by the lascars. These were usually in the form of playful questions asked by one set of men and answered by another group. Sadly, there is no record of these songs.

15 May

We have been busy, Mama and I. We have organized deck entertainment for the passengers. The captain says this helps keep them in good humour. So, Mama and I have got a few of the passengers together to put up a short play. The rehearsals take up most of our morning. It keeps us wonderfully busy and cheerful.

> Captains often travelled with their wives on board their ships. Although many sailors considered it bad luck to have women on board, the captain's wife usually helped her husband run the ship. Some women did the accounts, and others organized games and theatricals for the passengers on board.

21 May

The play was put up today. Mama has travelled with Papa before this and done all this. For me, all of this is fresh and new – the games and theatre. The captain had an awning put up on the deck for privacy during the play. Everyone remembered their lines and the audience laughed at all the right places. Halfway through the play, I looked up. And there, high above us, was a row of lascars, watching the play through a few holes in the awning. I said nothing. I only hoped watching the play would keep the lascars in good humour.

27 May
The captain warned us that we are approaching the Cape and bad weather lay ahead. This is the Cape of Good Hope, at the tip of Africa. Despite its name, it is known for its rough seas and stormy waves, and many ships have been wrecked here.

7 June
We have had a week of the captain's bad weather. There have been storms and high winds. The sea looks grey and turbulent, and the *Rosa Maria* has been thrown about on the waves. The lascars have worked without pause and

> The European sailors worked on 'watches' as shifts were called on ships. The lascars, on the other hand, were always all on duty. This meant that they did a lot more work than the other sailors on board the ship.

without fear, climbing the masts, taking in the sails. And when the water rushed into the hold, they spent hours bailing it out. They are the real heroes.

20 June
WET PAINT – this is what a lascar wrote in my notebook. I asked him to write something in my notebook, anything, to help me remember the lascars. He nodded and smiled, but I don't think he understood what I wanted. He looked in a very puzzled way at the notebook I held out to him. But I finally got him to understand. And then, after much thought, this is what he wrote – WET PAINT.

17 July
The captain says we have just crossed the Equator. The sailors got up a little celebration. One of them dressed up as Neptune, the Roman god of the sea. He sat in a chair as if it were a throne and the other sailors pulled his make-believe chariot along. If there was any man who had not crossed the line (the Equator), the sailors shaved his head. But there was no one like that on the ship, and I was glad.

The passengers all had little gifts for them, and the sailors seemed pleased by these. The captain says there's special food for them. The lascars don't get to eat that, though. Instead, they eat their usual meal. The captain says the dal is finished. Which means that the lascars only have rice.

Crossing the line was an important celebration aboard a ship. For the lascars though, the celebrations meant nothing since they did not eat the food that the other sailors enjoyed. However, they celebrated their own festivals and captains often permitted special food for the occasion.

29 July

The captain says the lascars eat thrice a day. But I have noticed that they only eat in the morning and at night. The captain says this is because the rice is almost finished. What little is still left is now black with mould.

And so, the lascars get smaller and smaller quantities of rice every day. While our table groans under the weight of different kinds of delicacies, the lascars are starving. The captain says I am making a fuss for nothing, and that the lascars are very happy to eat rice with spices. But the lascars don't look happy.

Food for the European sailors, officers and passengers on board a ship included live animals. These were slaughtered during the voyage. This meant that the Europeans rarely faced a shortage of food and fresh meat. The supplies meant for the lascars, however, often ran out. Captains of ships were convinced that lascars were happy to eat their minimal meals and rarely paid attention to these issues.

10 August

A lascar got into trouble today. The captain says it was his fault because he refused to obey orders. As punishment, he was dragged to the deck and tied there. The captain handed the *serang* a rope and asked him to give the lascar a flogging. The poor lascar screamed in fright, and all his friends broke into alarmed chatter. I shut my eyes when the *serang* raised his hand. But the *serang* didn't flog the lascar after all. I was glad and I could see that the lascars were relieved too. They made little jokes and large smiles flashed on their faces. The captain says this is a good way to get the lascars to work properly.

The *serang* was responsible for the lascars. This meant that lascars carried complaints to him. It also meant that he had to punish them when they broke rules. Many captains were terribly cruel to the lascars. They kept them tied for hours, starved them and flogged them.

17 August
The captain says we can expect cold weather soon. Everyone is already bundled up in shawls and coats. Except the lascars. They are still in their thin Indian pants and long shirts. The captain says the lascars can only work in hot weather. In the cold weather, they are useless. But I still see the lascars running around the ship, obeying the *serang*'s orders. Not one of them looked useless to me.

3 September
My lascar friend WET PAINT is ill. The captain says it is nothing, and the lascars like to pretend to be sick to shirk work. But I sneaked away to see him, and WET PAINT does not look like he is suffering from nothing. Or that he is pretending. He shivers all the time, and his face is pale. The lascars don't have a cabin like we do. All they have is a little space in the forecastle. It

The lascars were treated differently in terms of their food and salaries. They were also discriminated against in the sleeping space given to them. The European sailors were given 72 cubic feet of space, while lascars were given only 36 cubic feet. In 1913, this changed, and Europeans had 120 cubic feet while lascars were assigned 72 cubic feet. But the differential treatment continued. This was naturally not enough for them to sleep properly. The lascars had the space in the front of the ship, called the forecastle. This was small and cramped, with no ventilation and no light. In bad weather, the waves hit the front of the ship and the spray flew over the lascars huddled in their little space. Their clothes were constantly wet, with no place to dry them properly. Was it any surprise that they fell ill?

is not very pleasant because it is small and dark and sealed up.

The captain was angry with me for going there and even Mama said I had gone too far. But I had to know what happened to WET PAINT. The captain was surprised to hear the lascar's name. Surely, he said, it couldn't be his real name. I told him it wasn't. I had wondered about it too. Then one day, I saw the lascars painting the ship. One of them carefully printed out DO NOT TOUCH, and another WET PAINT. I knew then where my friend had found his name. But now I wanted to know his real name. The captain did not know. He said all lascars had strange names and knowing them didn't matter. But the captain is wrong. Names do matter.

Captains never bothered to find out the names of their lascar crew. Instead, the Europeans gave the lascars English names, often funny ones. Lascars took advantage of the fact that the captains didn't know or recognize them by hiding when they were in trouble. When the ship was close to the destination, these lascars would come out of hiding.

7 September
WET PAINT's real name is Bhoju, and he is dead. The *serang* told me his name and when I asked, his own name too, which is Lalji. He says the captain is to blame for Bhoju's death. Lalji is angry with the captain for not giving the lascars enough food. For the past month, they have had only rice twice a day. The vegetables are long gone, and there never was any lemon juice to give them. Serang Lalji is certain there will be more deaths.

Ships with lascars on them often had many deaths. Concerned, the directors of the East India Company appointed doctors to examine the lascars coming into England. William Hunter was one such doctor. He studied the cases of lascar deaths on several ships and identified lack of adequate food as the reason for these deaths. Scurvy was one of the diseases that struck the malnourished sailors. Scurvy caused swelling in the body and could lead to death. Dr Hunter made out a list of food items to be carried on board the ship. Lemon juice, long recognized as effective in preventing scurvy, was one of the items captains were supposed to give their crew.

10 September

Serang Lalji was right. More lascars have fallen ill. They shiver and mutter in their language, remembering the family they left behind in India. Sometimes, their legs swell like an ugly kind of gourd. The swelling travels up their bodies, past knees and thighs, to their stomachs and chest. They gasp for breath then. The captain has been giving them hot soup. But it is too late. They can barely swallow a mouthful before they begin to wheeze. The captain says there's nothing anyone can do about it. And everyone nods and agrees with him.

Ships were supposed to have a doctor on board. Where there was none, captains relied on doctors on passing ships. If that was not possible, the poor sailors had to suffer in silence and often died at sea. What about the families of the lascars in India? One of the duties of the *serang* was to ensure that the salary of a dead lascar was handed over to his family.

12 September

Five more lascars are dead. The captain says we will dock in London in 10 days.

20 September

The captain says we will reach London tomorrow, two days earlier than we expected. There is great excitement on the ship. People talk happily of being home again, of meeting their family after months away. They offer thanks for their safe passage home. They marvel that no one died on the long journey. It is all because of the captain, they say. But they are wrong. People have died on the ship. Fifteen lascars are dead and seven more are ill. And it is because of the captain.

21 September

We are home. The captain says we will stay here for the next year. (I can never think of him as Papa any more. He will be forever captain to me, the man who believes and says untrue things about the lascars and starves them.)

It is time, he says, that I get a little education and learn about the world.

He doesn't believe me when I tell him that I have already learnt many things about the world.

Or, that he is the one who taught them to me.

SECRET POST

HOW TO KEEP LASCARS HEALTHY WHILE ON A VOYAGE

Dr William Hunter studied the condition of many lascars who arrived on various ships from India. He used this study to put together suggestions on keeping lascars healthy, in a book. It said:

CLOTHING

The owners are obliged to give every sailor, who is a native of Asia or Africa, certain items of clothing. Part of these are to be provided in Bengal, and part in England.

Clothes to be given in Bengal:

- One jacket;
- A pair trousers, of red or blue cloth;
- A blanket;
- Two woollen caps;
- Two pairs of woollen gloves;
- One pair of shoes;
- One bed, made by sewing together three blankets;
- One pillow; and
- One canvas bag to carry all these.

Clothes to be given in England:

- One jacket;
- Two pairs trousers of woollen cloth;
- Two shirts;
- Two pairs socks;
- Two caps;
- Two pairs gloves;
- One pair shoes; and
- Every lascar should have a canvas hammock to sleep in.

SECRET POST

DIET

In addition to rice and dal, the lascars should be given these items daily -

- Garlic, onion, ginger, chillies, black pepper, ghee and turmeric.
- Vegetables such as pumpkin, yam, carrots and green vegetables can be preserved and carried on the ship.
- Sailors should be given enough water to drink. If it appears that they have scurvy, the water should be mixed with lime juice and given to sailors.

EXERCISE

- Cheerfulness is one of the greatest preservatives of health. Sports of various kind must be encouraged, when sailors are not on duty.
- Sailors enjoy music and so, a musician or two would be a useful addition to the crew.

CLEANLINESS ON THE SHIP

- The ports should be kept open in good weather. When the weather permits, beds should be carried on to the deck and aired properly.
- Lascars should not be allowed to keep on damp clothes or sleep in them. They should be asked to change at once into dry clothes. In cold climates, if the blankets provided are not sufficient, they should be given blue shirts to keep warm.

9

HOW MANY LASCARS DOES A SHIP NEED?

On 28 February 1802, the *Union* completed the journey from Bengal to London. Unlike many of the ships that were in the port, the *Union* was not owned by the East India Company. It was a country ship.

On 24 March 1802, William Docker visited the ship and examined the lascars on board. William Docker was the East India Company's medical superintendent.

> When the East India Company began to trade with India, they needed many ships to transport the goods they carried for the English markets. Several of the ships that plied between the two countries were owned by the East India Company. The others were owned by individuals or companies, and were given a licence to ply in the trading zone of the East India Company. These ships were called country ships.

He reported that several lascars had died at sea and that many others were ill. He presented his findings to the shipping committee of directors and also suggested that the *Union* be investigated.

In the years since the Company began trading with India, more and more lascars were employed on ships. Many lascars died on the long journey and many others fell seriously ill. The company appointed William Docker in 1798 and a resident surgeon named William Hunter in 1801. William Hunter wrote a book titled *An Essay on the Diseases Incident to Indian Seamen, or Lascars on Long Voyages*. This was based on his report on the condition of the lascars on ships that had docked in London. He identified the diseases the lascars suffered and suggested the food ship captains could carry to ensure that their lascars stayed healthy.

Mir Jahan was the *serang* of the *Union*. When asked to report on the voyage, Mir Jahan informed the committee that the *Union* had sailed from Bengal with a crew of seventy-four. Not all of these men were experienced sailors. Only around 60 had sailed before. Twenty-eight of these men died during the voyage. This meant that

A ship the size of the *Union* required at least 100 men to sail it. This was because the sailors were expected to have time to rest between their shifts. This would keep them alert and help them react quickly in an emergency.

only 32 lascars did the actual work to keep the *Union* sailing. The committee was shocked.

How did the owner of the *Union* allow the ship to sail with such a small crew? And what about Captain Luke? He must have known that the ship needed many experienced sailors to make the voyage and reach its destination safely. These questions remained unanswered.

Employing lascars cost much less than recruiting English sailors. So, captains were eager to appoint lascars. However, the East India Company charged the captains 14 pounds per lascar. This money was meant to cover the cost of looking after the lascars when they were in England and sending them home again. Captains tried to cut costs by appointing fewer lascars than they needed.

The committee talked to Mir Jahan and to several lascars. All of them complained about Captain Luke and his officers. According to Mir Jahan, these men had beaten the lascars badly. The beatings had begun soon after the ship had sailed out of Bengal, leaving many of the men injured. They fell ill as a result and were not able to attend to their regular duties. This gave the captain more reason to beat them, this time for not working. The men tried to escape the beating by sneaking away to the hold. They possibly also hoped to get some much-needed rest. But the captain found them and this time, he beat Mir Jahan for not controlling his lascars.

The condition of the lascars worsened over the days. They were not given proper beds to sleep in. Instead, they were expected to sleep on the deck. The constant spray of the salt water caused their clothes to stay damp and worsened their condition.

Lascars who were treated badly on the voyage often lodged complaints against the captain and officers of the ship when they reached London. The East India Company took these complaints seriously and investigated them thoroughly. The lascars of the *Union*

This was the age of sail and ships relied on strong winds to help them move. This meant that the crew had to constantly be on the alert, managing the sails so the ship could sail smoothly. The sails had to be raised and lowered in order to keep the ship on course and safe. That is why it was necessary for every ship to have a sufficient number of lascars to help steer the ship.

had the support of John Moore, one of the junior officers on the ship. Moore refused to join the captain and the other officers in beating the lascars. This annoyed the captain and as punishment, Moore was not given food for three days.

John Moore tried to stand up against the captain and the officers. When the ship halted at St. Helena, he

Why did the lascars sleep on the deck?

The ship was inspected before it sailed from Bengal. It is possible that the captain allowed the lascars to sleep in their proper berths at this time. Once the inspection was completed, the lascars were expected to sleep on the deck.

even wrote a letter to the governor about the terrible treatment of the lascars on board the *Union*. However, nothing came of this brave attempt, except that the angry captain made things difficult for Moore.

More than two dozen lascars died on the journey to London. The remaining crew was now ready to stand with Moore and lodge a complaint against Captain Luke and the other officers. The lawyer for the East India Company agreed that Moore and the lascars had a real cause for complaint. It was decided that both Captain Luke and another officer named Plumb would be punished. But both of them left England before this could happen.. These men could only be prosecuted if they returned to England. Even then, they would not be charged with murder, even though they had killed so

Starving lascars was a way to punish them for bad behaviour. It was rare to hear of a situation where an English sailor was punished in a similar manner. The lascars on the ship, on the other hand, must have been starved on several counts. Added to their ill-health, this period of starvation made them weaker, and unable to carry out their jobs properly.

many men. At the most, the captain would be accused of not hiring a doctor to travel on the *Union*.

How could such cruel men as Captain Luke and Officer Plumb get away so easily?

The captain of the *Union* was expected to follow three rules. He had to ensure that there was a doctor on board the ship; he had to give the lascars roomy, healthy space to stay in; and have the ship inspected by the master-attendant before it set out on its journey. Since he had fulfilled these, he could not legally be punished. That's how cruel captains got away even when it was proved that they were guilty.

Does that mean that the tragic deaths of the lascars was forgotten?

No, it was not forgotten. In the future, the captains of ships had to give a written explanation for the death of lascars on the journey. This was meant to ensure that the lascars were protected and the voyage did not turn into a fatal one for them.

10

WHAT ABOUT THE LASCARS?

The people of Dunkirk, in France, have a new hero. His name is Captain Robert Eastwick and he is the owner of the ship *Elizabeth*, which was recently wrecked off the Dunkirk coast. Every day, people invite Captain Eastwick to dinner and shower praise on him. They all want to hear the story of how he managed to escape the storm. They know nothing of the lascars on board the ship. And so, they don't ask about them. But I do. And I want to ask Captain Eastwick, *what about the lascars?*

I first met Captain Eastwick in November 1810, when I bought my passage on the *Elizabeth*. Captain Eastwick had recently bought shares in the ship and he was travelling on it. The ship was going from London to Calcutta. There were 30 cabin passengers and I was one of them. There were also 300 lascars. But 256 of these were passengers on the ship.

We left London in November 1810, and right from the beginning, the elements were against us. There was

Wait, weren't lascars sailors? Then why were lascars travelling as passengers on the *Elizabeth*?

Remember that ships travelling from India to England hired lascars to make the journey. When the ship reached London, the lascars joined all the others, who like them, had travelled from India. They were all waiting for a job on a ship going to India. This was difficult and took time. And so, the number of lascars in England increased. At such times, the East India Company bought them tickets and sent them back to India. That was how these 256 lascars were travelling as passengers on the *Elizabeth*.

a heavy wind blowing. This made it difficult for the crew to get the ship into Portsmouth harbour. When we got there, we stayed for a few days because the captain was hoping the weather would change. But we had no luck. Bad weather followed us when we set sail again and, then, the *Elizabeth* developed a leak. This was worrying, but the captain managed to get us to Cork in Ireland. We waited there for some time. Repairs were carried out on the ship, and more passengers boarded. Twenty of these were lascars. For the next week, we had good weather and sailing was pleasant.

Not for long, though. It seemed like we were cursed because we ran into stormy weather once more and the ship sprung a leak again. And then, the ship began to fill up with water. The hold had about four-and-a-half feet of water. Why, there was about three feet of water on the deck too. All the passengers were bundled up in warm clothes and kept to their cabins.

But what about the lascars? They had no warm clothes and I saw them shiver in the intense cold. Why, I wondered, didn't they go down into the hold? Even with the water there, they would be sheltered from the cold wind.

Remember all those stories that captains of ships believed about lascars? One of these was that lascars liked to sleep on the deck. Not everyone accepted this, and a traveller named Robert Minturn made a sarcastic note in his book about how lascars were not usually provided a place to sleep, because they are 'allowed to select the softest planks as a bed'.

Still, in this case, asking the lascars to sleep on the deck was shocking. They were not working on the *Elizabeth*. They were paying customers who had tickets to travel home. It was cruel to keep them on the deck in the biting cold weather.

For two days, the passengers huddled in their cabins, with water sloshing about. The captain tried to get the lascars to go on deck and work. But how could they do it when they were so cold and wet?

These were probably the lascars who worked on the *Elizabeth*. But even when the lascars travelled as passengers on a ship, captains expected them to work. The *serangs* refused to let the lascars work and there were many arguments with the captain of the ship.

The weather turned so rough that the ship was forced to turn back to England. Everyone on board was worried and frightened. Captain Eastwick talked to us often, and he always seemed very cheerful. We felt better after this.

But what about the lascars? I never saw him talk to them or assure them that everything was going to be all right, and that they would soon be back home.

Then, the *Elizabeth* ran aground in the middle of the night. We felt the sudden shock as the bottom of the ship scraped on the sandbar. There were screams of fear as people rushed about. When I went on the deck, I saw that the *Elizabeth* was stuck fast on a sandbar. The lascars were terrified, and their frightened voices reached me. But no one calmed them down. Instead, the passengers seemed to be afraid that the lascars would take over all the available space on the deck. To my horror, I saw them grab any weapon that lay close at hand and swing it at the lascars. I saw swords and sticks used to threaten them. The poor lascars darted about, trying to get to a place where they could be safe. But the weapons kept them back.

I heard the boom of the ship's guns. They were fired to attract the people on the land. Perhaps someone would come out in a boat to save us! But the wind was too strong, and the rain made it impossible to see clearly. If we wanted to live, we had to save ourselves. And so, the captain helped to launch a boat full of people. But the waves dashed against it and it was destroyed. All the people in it were swept away by the waves.

'The only thing we can do now,' Captain Eastwick said, 'is for a few of us to take another boat and seek help from the people on the mainland.' The wind howled and threw the rain at us, the waves pounded the sides of the ship and rushed over to wash the decks. How could anyone expect to make it safely through this storm?

'Who will volunteer to go with me?' Captain Eastwick asked, looking around.

Silence was the only response. I looked around and saw fear on every face. Then one man came forward... and another.

The sailors got the boat ready and Captain Eastwick stood by it, waiting for more volunteers. To all of us, the ship seemed the safest place at the moment. Who would want to be on the stormy sea, with the waves throwing up great walls of water? At that moment, one of the lascars pushed through the crowd and got into the boat. He called out something and other lascars rushed to join him.

'Hey, you,' Captain Eastwick shouted. 'Stop!' But there was no stopping the lascars. Ten or 12 of them were now in the boat. At this, the captain picked up an oar and began to beat them off.

'Out!' he shouted. 'Get out of the boat!' Hadn't he just asked for more volunteers? Besides, there seemed to be plenty of room on the boat for the lascars.

'Captain,' I called, 'why don't you let them sail on the boat with you?'

'You don't know these men,' the captain gasped, still swinging his oar around. 'If I don't stop them, they will certainly swamp us here!'

A few of the women protested, and I raised my voice too. But there was no stopping the captain. He beat the men until they got out of the boat.

'We will bring back help,' the captain said as the boat was finally launched.

We stood on the deck of the *Elizabeth*, gazing hopefully after the boat. But the lascars were huddled together in a corner. They knew there was no hope for them. Any boat that came for help, they knew, would not have room for them. Even with danger threatening us, I knew that the captain had not been fair. He should have talked to the lascars; he should have taken a few of them on the boat. But he didn't and now they are dead. And the people of Dunkirk know nothing of this. All they know is that they have found a new hero. And his name is Captain Robert Eastwick.

Was Captain Eastwick able to bring back help for the people on the ship?

No, the sea was too rough for any boat to come back for help. So the people on the *Elizabeth* stayed there. Three more boats were launched from the *Elizabeth*, and the people on it managed to make it ashore. But the *Elizabeth* was wrecked before help could come and all the remaining people on board were killed. This included 310 lascars.

TWO CUPBOARDS AND SALTED FISH

What happened to the lascars once they reached London? The owners of the ships were supposed to take care of them but seldom did. So, the East India Company built depots where these men could rest between voyages. Did these places provide good living quarters for the lascars? Let's find out!

Albert Todd was the youngest of the staff in the office. He was also the newest and had been in his job only a week. In that time, Albert had carried cups of tea and messages into various offices.

Something big, Albert knew, was going to happen that day. There had been a flurry of messages the day before and two urgent meetings. But Albert knew no details. All he knew was that it was something to do with lascars. He was faintly puzzled by it. He knew about lascars and had sometimes seen them begging on the streets. But why would important people worry about lascars?

To Albert, like to many other citizens of England, lascars were only the beggars they saw in tattered clothes on street corners. But lascars mattered to many different people in the country and out of it. To the English businessmen who sent ships to India, lascars were the cheap and easily available crew who brought their ships back to England. To the captains of these ships, lascars were the people who could be expected to work hard on the voyage and then be abandoned in England. For the directors of the East India Company, lascars were a source of anxiety. Since the lascars were brought to England on Company ships, they felt a sense of responsibility for them. The Company was constantly trying to find ways to make sure that the lascars did not cause problems for the people of England.

Albert didn't expect to learn more. After all, he was the youngest and newest member of the staff. But he was in for a surprise when he walked into his little office that morning.

'Mr Todd,' the head of the Parliamentary Committee of Enquiry said, 'you will accompany us and make notes of our observations.'

Where was this committee going? And why?

Over the years, the number of lascars brought into England had risen. The owners of the ships they came on were supposed to arrange accommodation for them until they could go home to India. But most owners did not bother to do this. As a result, London was teeming with lascars driven to beg on the streets. The Company was forced to make arrangements for a place for the lascars to live in while they were in London.

The Company had contracts with different people over the years to house the lascars in the city. The first of these depots was started in 1797 in Shoreditch in London. But the local people objected to the problems caused by the presence of the lascars and so the depot was moved to Ratcliffe Highway in 1799, where it was run by Mr Abraham Gole, and later his son.

In February 1814, two social reformers who visited Gole's depot were horrified at the conditions in which the lascars lived. They founded the Society for the Protection of Asiatic Sailors and published the details of their visit in the form of a letter in *The Times* newspaper. As a result, in 1815, the Parliament set up a 'Committee on Lascars and other Asiatic Seamen' to investigate the lascar issue. The members of this committee were going to inspect Mr Abraham Gole's depot for seamen.

A sheaf of papers was thrust into Albert Todd's hands, along with a pen. He stared at them. And then, as the five members of the committee walked away, he leapt to life and followed them.

The East India Company did everything they could to provide for the lascars. They asked the owners of the ships to take care of lascars in England. They asked shipowners to buy a bond for every lascar on board their ships. However, nothing worked, and lascars continued to complain that shipowners did not care for them while the people of London objected to the presence of lascars. Finally, in 1795, the Company took on the responsibility of maintaining the lascars in England.

From the Notes of Albert Todd

1. On 5 November 1815, a surprise visit was made to the depot where lascars were housed.
2. The depot was located on Ratcliffe Highway and run by Mr Abraham Gole.
3. The purpose was to inspect the depot to see if it was maintained well.
4. The depot was constructed on a large parcel of land. There was a tall wall around the building.

5. A notice beside the gate informed visitors that it was kept locked between 11 p.m. and 6 a.m.
6. No information had been sent to Mr Gole about the inspection. It was meant to be a surprise inspection. (But that Mr Gole, he didn't look surprised. He looked shocked!)
7. Mr Gole led the way in and showed us around. (He didn't look very happy about it, though!)
8. The depot had many large rooms. The crew of a ship, Mr Gole said, liked to stay together in one room.
9. The committee members peeped into several rooms. Each had a small stove for the sailors to cook food.
10. The committee members noticed that the rooms were all completely bare, with no furniture at all. (The lascars liked it this way, Mr Gole told us. But surely no one would like to lie on the cold floor?)
11. The committee members saw several lascars lying on the bare ground. They did not have a blanket or any kind of bedding.
12. The committee members demanded an explanation from Mr Gole. (Many of them looked furious. It was only their manners that stopped them from shaking Mr Gole!)
13. This is what Mr Gole told them:
    - The lascars were given bedding on the ship. But they sold it as soon as the voyage was over.

This was just one of the many stories that were popular about the lascars, that they didn't need furniture in their rooms. The rooms in Gole's depot, therefore, had no furniture and were not heated. The European sailors, on the other hand, were housed in Gole's own home. They were given better food and treated well too. The large number of lascar deaths was usually attributed to the general weakness and ill-health of the lascars.

- The lascars were given warm clothes too – two flannel-lined trousers, a coat, stockings and a cap, all of which they also sold.
- Not being used to the cold weather of England, they fell ill.

These, Mr Gole said, were the people the committee had seen sleeping on the floor. These lascars needed to see a doctor. But they refused to be parted from their friends and so they stayed on in the depot.

14. The committee members were not convinced by Mr Gole's arguments. (I was not, either. It sounded like a whole bundle of excuses.) One committee member asked him why he could not give the lascars a fresh set of warm clothes and bedding.

Gole was right about the lascars selling their bedding and clothes, but he did not bother to explain why they were forced to do this. It was because they had no money for food. Many captains turned the lascars away without giving them their pay. Others kept the lascars waiting for days before they finally paid them. The lascars had to eat and so they sold whatever they had. Most ships from India reached England in fall, which meant that the lascars had to live through the cold winter without adequate warm clothes. When they fell ill and needed treatment, the lascars, frightened in a foreign environment, refused to leave their friends and go into a hospital. This meant that they could not be isolated, and diseases often spread among all the members of the crew.

'Because,' Mr Gole said, 'they will sell them too!'

The committee members did not appear to like this answer. (I did not, either. It sounded like the weakest kind of excuse.)

'Please remember, Mr Gole,' one of the committee members said, 'you have been appointed to take care of these poor souls.'

'And I do!' Mr Gole said. 'I take very good care of them.'

Gole was paid a fixed amount by the Company for the lascars under his care. For just five months in 1813-14, Gole was paid 13,804 pounds. Gole, on his part, said he gave the lascars so much food that they sold it to make money.

15. No one believed him. The depot was dark and very dirty. The rooms were overcrowded, and a thick smell hung in the rooms and corridors. It was the odour of dirty clothes, and crowding of people, and illness.
16. Mr Gole saw that the members of the committee did not believe him. And that made him angry. He threw open a door and invited us to inspect the room. The lascars in the room were cooking something on a little stove.
17. 'Look,' Mr Gole said, 'this is what each lascar gets.' There was rice, dal, salt, spices, onions, tamarind and salted fish. Mr Gole said the lascars liked to curry it.

    'But my good man, why?' he was asked. 'Fresh fish is easily available in London. Why, it is the cheapest meat available!'

    'But salted fish is good for them!' Mr Gole said.
18. It was obvious to the members of the committee (and to me too) that Mr Gole was simply making

excuses. So, the members ignored him and asked one of the lascars how he was. The lascar nodded and smiled happily. He was sitting between two tall cupboards with locks on them.

19. 'What is in those?' a member asked.

'Probably clothes,' was Mr Gole's reply. But he had just told us that the lascars sold their clothes and bedding. Then what did they keep in a cupboard?

The lascar was asked to open the cupboard. He unlocked it and out walked a lascar. When the

The committee members had a point. With fresh fish so easily available, why were the lascars given salted fish? Gole used one of the many prevailing theories about lascars to cut down on food costs so he could increase his own profits. In June 1813, he asked for an increase in the fixed amount he received from the Company, but was refused.

second cupboard was unlocked, there was a lascar in there too! The *serang* had put them in there as punishment for quarrelling.

The *serang* was responsible for the well-being of the lascars as well as disciplining them. It was easy for people like Gole to simply allow the *serang* to do as they liked, rather than intervene.

20. The committee members walked around the depot, observing everything. And when they finally walked away, Mr Gole stood watching them. A bad report would cause him trouble. A good one would mean that the questions and surprise visits would end.
21. The committee members were talking among themselves as they walked away. One of them said something in a loud voice and the words reached Mr Gole. 'Two cupboards of lascars and salted fish!' the voice said. 'That's terrible!'
22. Mr Gole sighed and his shoulders sagged. He knew now what kind of report he could expect. No surprises about that.

The committee made several observations based on their visit to the depot. They recommended that

Gole was optimistic to think so! The question of the lascars continued to trouble England for several years. Since they could not be hired as sailors on ships going to India, they were sent as passengers by the Company, which paid for their tickets. But often, the captains of the ships expected them to work on the voyage. The *serangs* objected to working without pay and so this ploy failed too.

the East India Company build new quarters for the lascars, in an area close to the docks. They also felt the need to have a supervisor who had some knowledge and experience of the lascars' home country. The East India Company was asked to keep a close eye on the running of the depot and make efforts to send the stranded lascars home at the earliest.

Was this new depot ever built? Unfortunately, no. The Company flatly refused to build the depot and urged the British government to do it instead. The government, which had always held the Company responsible for lascars, made no move to build these quarters, either. The East India Dock Company suggested that the lascars should be

Lascars waiting to go home often took up jobs in London. However, this threatened the local people since they lost their jobs to the outsiders. When the lascars tried to earn some money by unloading ships, they got into trouble with the Englishmen who usually did this job. This resulted in fights that only showed the lascars in a bad light.

housed in large boats that would be moored in the river Thames. But this proposal fell through and no attempts were made to build new living quarters for the lascars.

In 1834, the Parliament suspended the East India Company's right to trade in India for the next 20 years. This meant that the Company was no longer responsible for the lascars. They immediately closed down the depot run by Abraham Gole.

However, lascars continued to pour into England. The sight of the poor lascars bothered many kind-hearted English people, and they did their best to provide these men with food and clothes. In 1856, The Strangers' Home for Asiatics, Africans and South Sea Islanders was set up in London, with donations collected from people. Duleep Singh, the maharaja of Punjab, made one of the largest donations, giving 500 rupees towards the building of the home. Here, sailors from different parts of the world could find a place to stay while they waited for a passage home. But not every sailor wanted to return home. Some of them opened small businesses in England, married local women and settled there.

12

A LASCAR'S TALE - ACROSS MILES AND YEARS

When we woke up one morning and found you gone, we were surprised. We all remembered how, the previous night, you had taken very little rice so your brothers would get more. It was the memory of this very small mound of rice on your plate that made us think that you had woken up hungry. But where could you have gone? The trees outside were bare and there was nothing in any of the fields that could be eaten.

It was your grandmother who said, 'That Bholo, I know where he has gone.'

'Where?' we all asked.

'He's gone to fish,' she told us.

You were always her favourite, and she knew you well.

'Oh, yes,' we nodded. After all, you were our oldest boy and you had quick eyes. You must have seen how your mother never ate with us. Perhaps you had seen the little mouthful that she ate at every meal. And so, you must have woken up early to fish in the river.

Your mother rushed to light the fire. 'Fetch me some firewood,' she called to your brothers. 'I will cook a little rice to eat with Bholo's fish.'

The news of your fish acted like magic on everyone. Your grandmother said she would help cook the meal. I went out to see if I could find anything worth eating in the fields. A handful of potatoes that we had overlooked, perhaps. But there was nothing there. How could anything grow without water? Everywhere I looked I saw the empty fields, brown and dusty. Even the tall trees had lost their greenness, which was hidden under layers of reddish brown dust. It was difficult to feel hopeful in a landscape like this.

There would be fish to eat, I reminded myself. Bholo would have to walk for hours to get to the river, but he would bring us some fish.

Your brothers came running just then. 'Bholo,' they panted. 'Bholo has run away! He has gone away to sign up on a ship.'

You, a sailor? Why? You are a farmer. You are tied to the land. How could you forget that? What drove you to the sea?

Your mother and grandmother broke into loud weeping. The noise brought the neighbours running. They calmed us down. Our Bholo, they said, is a responsible boy. He will

Many of the men who signed up to work on a ship were farmers. When the rains failed, the number of men travelling from villages to take up work on a ship increased. Driven by hunger, these men hoped to make some money working as lascars before they returned home.

earn some money and come running back home. They remembered stories of others who had left the village and gone to sea. Many of them had returned years later, with enough money to buy their families all luxuries.

'Your Bholo will be back soon,' they told us. 'And your problems will be over then.'

Your salary and all the things we would buy with it – all that was in the future. For now, we could not stop thinking of you and wondering where you were and how you were.

In the mid-eighteenth century, the salary of a lascar was between 12 and 18 shillings. Experienced sailors were paid well. Of course, Bholo could not expect to earn that much. After all, he knew nothing at all about ships and sailing. But for a farmer whose crops had failed, even this small amount would make a big difference.

All your mother could wonder was, 'But why did Bholo run away?' The only one who could have answered that question was you and you were not there. And so, after a while your mother said, 'He is only a boy. Perhaps Bholo will not get a job.' She looked around at us. 'Why,' she asked us, 'would anyone give a farmer's son a job on a ship?'

We jumped eagerly on that hope. After all, you had lived all your life in the village of Duldua. You had never stepped beyond the limits of the village. You had never gone to Calcutta and you had never seen the sea. How could a boy like this be of any use on a ship?

'He'll come home soon,' your grandmother said. She dragged her cot outside and set it in the shade of the tree. There she sat all day, eyes fixed on the road.

'I am waiting for Bholo,' she told everyone. 'He will come home soon!'

Bholo's family was right – he knew nothing at all about sailing a ship. But they didn't know that captains of ships were always in need of men. Without enough sailors, they could not set sail for England. The *ghat serangs* knew this too, and they often signed on men with no experience at sea or of sailing. Sometimes, *ghat serangs* even kidnapped men and forced them to work on ships.

Days passed and months. The sun shone down and your grandmother was forced to drag her cot back into the house. Now she said nothing about waiting for you. Instead, she lay on her cot, sighing and muttering to herself. 'He is all alone, that boy,' we heard her say. 'How will he manage without anyone to look after him?'

The rains arrived then. Our brown fields were covered with a carpet of green. Everyone heaved a sigh of relief. It was a busy time of planting and watching over the crops that grew taller and stronger each day. If only, we thought, if only Bholo had waited.

The rains stopped and the sky turned a clear blue. It was time for your grandmother to drag her cot outside. But she had stopped waiting for you. She no longer watched the road or asked about you. Still, she never stopped thinking about you. When winter came, she remembered how much you had loved the season. Were you feeling the cold bite of a winter wind, wherever you were? And did it remind you of home?

Ships that sailed from India usually left in spring and reached England in winter. Bholo's ship was probably sailing closer and closer to London. The journey would have been a challenging one, with storms causing damage and delay. Often, ships were wrecked by these storms. In the first 20 years of the East India Company, less than half its ships returned from Asia. Between 1700 and 1818, as many as 160 ships of the Company sank or were captured.

It is now a year since you went away. We miss you still and talk of you often. Your grandmother lies on her cot all day. Sometimes, she says, 'If only we heard from Bholo. A message, a token, just a sign will do!'

We have been over the numbers so often! Nine months to sail from Calcutta to London. Two or three months to

Once a ship sailed away, it was impossible to get in touch with a lascar. Lascars were unlettered, so they would not have known what to make of a letter. After they boarded a ship, lascars were rarely known by their own names. The English officers of the ship found it difficult to remember Indian names. And so, they gave the lascars nicknames that the Englishmen found easy to remember.

find a new job. And nine more months to sail back to Calcutta. The answer is always the same – it is now time you came home.

There are times when it seems that you will never come home. So many things have happened, so many things have changed that perhaps you will not want to come home. All we want is a sign that you are well. If only we had that, we think, we would be at peace.

There were a number of possibilities to explain why Bholo had not returned home. On reaching London, it is possible that he would have spent his salary. That would have left him with no money. Like many other desperate lascars, Bhola too might have started begging on the streets.

Or he might have left London and travelled around England. It was also possible that he married an Englishwoman and settled down in England. Occasionally, he would have thought of home and the little village where he had lived all his life. He must have told himself that he would go back one day. But it is likely that he never did. That he lived in England and died of old age. And that Bholo of Duldua village was buried in a corner of a graveyard in England.

13

THE STORY OF JULIAN

Once upon a time, there was a boy with big, black eyes and teeth that shone white. His hair curled crisply, and when he smiled, strangers turned into friends. The boy lived with his mother in a little house in a city called Madras. The boy's mother went to the market every day to sell vegetables. The boy stayed at home and played with his friends. As he grew older, he did

> Early English travellers to India often brought back Indian servants. In the seventeenth century, Indian domestic help added to the prestige of a household. Why, even the king of England, Charles II, asked for servants from India! In 1638, King Charles II made a very specific demand, asking the East India Company to provide him with one male and two female servers from India.

small jobs, and by the time he was 10 years old, he was earning money regularly.

One day, a Sahib saw the boy sitting outside his house.

'Will you work for me?' the Sahib asked. Everyone knew that sahibs were rich and paid well. The boy jumped to his feet, eager to start work. And so, when the Sahib asked him to get into a carriage, the boy did as he was told.

The door was slammed shut and the carriage began to move. 'Sahib,' the boy called. 'Sahib, won't you get in?' There was no reply.

When the boy tried to open the door of the carriage, he could not. It was locked. Then the boy knew what had happened. He had been Stolen. His mother had warned him to stay away from strangers. And he had not listened to her. He was trapped now! The boy shivered to think what the Sahib would do to him.

> This was Captain Dawes. There are records of Captain Dawes taking a young boy from Madras to England in 1720. However, there is very little other information about either the boy or Captain Dawes.

Would he shout at him? Or beat him? The Sahib did neither. He took the boy into a house where the boy was given new clothes to wear and good food to eat. He could wander around the house and the garden, but he was not allowed to go out. When he tried to slip out of the gate, the *chowkidar* stopped him. The wall around the house was too high and, in any case, there was a gardener also around to stop him.

The English usually entered into a contract with the Indian servants they employed. There are, however, accounts of Indians who were taken to England without any kind of contract. In the case of Julian, it is unclear whether he was taken to England with his mother's permission.

Another Englishman, William Hickey, purchased an Indian boy named Munoo and took him to England. He was educated in England and settled down there.

William Hickey's friend, John Auriol, had purchased a young boy whom he had named Nabob. In 1779, when Hickey was looking for a servant to accompany him to England, Auriol gave him Nabob, as a gift. This young boy was a great favourite with Hickey's family and even attended school while in England. Interestingly, when Hickey returned to India a few years later, Auriol claimed Nabob and took him away. This lack of a servant's control over his own life was frightening but was accepted in the society of the time.

One day, the Sahib took the boy on a ship. The only way the boy could escape now was by jumping off the ship. But the boy could not swim. So, he did nothing at all. The ship let out a long hoot and began to move. The movement of the ship made him sick, and he cried out for his mother. As the days passed, though, the boy got used to the ship. He still missed his mother and there were times when he cried for her.

Indians who were taken away from their homes and families often had a difficult time adjusting to their new life in England. Most of them spoke little English and were usually lonely. A British household in India employed several servants, each in charge of one particular job. But once these servants were taken to England, they were expected to take on other responsibilities.

There was much to see in the new country the ship sailed to. The boy stared at the buildings and the people, their clothes, and the carriages on the road. This was London and this was going to be his home now. The Sahib took him to meet a memsahib who lived in a big house full of people. Her name was Mrs Turner and she was very interested in the boy. She shook hands with him, checked his teeth and asked him to walk across the room. 'Good, good,' she said many times.

When she had finished asking him questions, she said, 'And now, you will stay with me and work for me.' The Sahib left the boy with Mrs Turner and went away.

At first, the boy was scared, but Mrs Turner was kind to him. She gave him new clothes and shoes. The boy had a new name too – Julian.

'Julian, Julian,' Mrs Turner called all day long. Julian didn't mind the new name and he liked the new clothes. But he didn't like it when Mrs Turner said, 'Speak, Julian. Say something in your language!' Speaking in his language made him homesick and reminded him of his mother. 'Dance,' Mrs Turner often said. 'Dance in the Indian style, Julian.'

English employers of Indian help exploited their exotic appeal, dressing them in Indian clothes and expecting them to dance or sing in the Indian way. The Countess of Londesborough had an Indian page called Bimbi. When she held parties, Bimbi, dressed in Indian clothes, was expected to direct the guests.

Julian remembered the way people had danced during festivals at home. And he whirled around, arms twisting and waving. 'Wonderful,' Mrs Turner clapped. 'Now, sing a song, Julian, an Indian song.' Julian sang the song he had heard women sing in the temple near his house. His voice was loud and not always tuneful. But Mrs Turner seemed to enjoy it.

At first, Julian was glad to see her smile and hear her cries of joy. But he soon grew to hate it. Every time Mrs Turner had a visitor, she sent for Julian. 'Sing for us, Julian,' she said. 'Dance for us.' She bought him fancy Indian clothes, decorated with gold lace. Julian disliked those clothes. He dreaded being called by Mrs Turner and hearing her say, 'Dance in the Indian way, Julian!' The other servants said he was lucky that Mrs Turner liked him so much. But Julian thought he was the unluckiest person in the world.

Mrs Turner apparently believed that she had treated Julian with great kindness. This is probably because she compared his situation in India with the comforts he enjoyed in her home. She seemed not to have understood that Julian disliked being made to perform at her bidding.

One day, when he could not take it any longer, Julian decided to escape. He waited until Mrs Turner was asleep.

One by one, he heard the other servants go to bed. When he was certain everyone was asleep, Julian lit a candle. But what if someone saw the light? Julian quickly pushed the candle under his bed. Now, there was enough light for him to see. By the dim glow, he pulled on his clothes. Then he crept carefully down the stairs.

He was afraid someone would hear him. But no one did, and Julian sighed with relief. Now all he had to do was open the large front door. This took a little time because Julian had to open it slowly and gently, so that no one in the house would hear it creak. When it was open, Julian stepped out and took a deep breath of the night air. Finally, he was free.

Julian ran down the street. All the other houses were in darkness and there was no one to see him go. At the end of the street, Julian turned for one last look at the house that had turned him into a performing monkey. To his horror, he saw that the house was up in flames. Julian stared at the orange flames hungrily eating chunks out of the house. He remembered then the candle he had pushed under his bed and knew a moment of regret.

His carelessness had started the fire. Faint cries came to his ears, cries of horror and fear. Should he go and help? But if he went back now, Julian knew he would never be able to flee again. He would have to go back

to his life as a prisoner, singing and dancing when Mrs Turner asked him to. Julian shut his ears to the shouts of the people in the house, turned his back on the flames and ran.

Did Julian live happily ever after?

Unfortunately, no. Julian was soon caught by the authorities, and accused of stealing money from Mrs Turner and setting fire to her house. He was found guilty and hanged to death.

SECRET POST

SHAMPOO AMBASSADOR

A few Indians who came to England married local women, set up their own businesses and settled down. The most famous of these was a man named Sake Dean Mahomed. At a young age, Dean Mahomed began to work for Godfrey Baker, who served in the Company's Bengal Army. When Baker left the army to return to Ireland, Dean Mahomed went with him. He learnt English, married and in 1794 published *The Travels of Dean Mahomet*, the first book written in English by an Indian. In 1810, he set up the Hindoostanee Coffee-House in London. Around 1814, he moved to Brighton to set up the Indian Vapour Baths and Shampooing Establishment in Brighton. He achieved great success with this and was soon appointed the Shampooing Surgeon to King George IV.

In fact, the English word '**shampoo**' comes from the terms *champoo*, ***champi***, ***champy*** or *champna*, which refer to a head massage, with some kind of oil, in Hindi and other north Indian languages.

14

LOOKING FOR A SERVANT

One bright morning in 1795, the Neville family gathered in the living room of their house. Mrs Neville had a thick bundle of newspapers. 'Mr Neville, Thomas, Martha...I want everyone to help me,' she announced.

'But, Mama,' her son Thomas said. 'Why aren't Lucy and Grace here?'

'Because they are too young to be of any use,' their mother told him. 'Now, come on, let's get to work.' Thomas picked up a newspaper and handed another to his sister. The Neville family lived in London and they were looking for a new servant for their home. They turned the pages of the newspapers, looking carefully at the advertisements there. 'Look!' Mrs Neville said. 'This looks promising!'

> A Black man from Bengal, having spent the last 20 years here, is looking for a good house. He was brought from India by his master and has served faithfully all these years.

The English families who had lived in India were used to a large army of servants. They often brought several of them out to England with them. The Indians who had lived for a few years in England not only picked up some English, but also other skills. The most important of these was the ability to advertise themselves. When they needed a new job, they placed advertisements in the newspapers, listing their qualifications and seeking new employers. It's sad that they needed to describe themselves in racist terms as 'black'.

'Hmm,' Mr Neville said, 'if he has already worked for 20 years…he may be too old to work for us.'

His wife looked doubtful, but before she could say anything, Mr Neville said, 'Look at this one.'

An East Indian is looking for a job with a single gentleman or even a small family. He can read, write and do simple accounts, can clean furniture and look after horses too.

'But we are not a small family,' Mrs Neville objected. 'There are four children and two adults. I wonder if we will find someone looking for a job in a big family!'

What did the English look for in the people they employed? The Indians who had spent years working for the English, knew this well. Women listed the ability to cook, clean, sew and look after their mistress as accomplishments. For men, it was the ability to read and write. Having travelled and being able to speak a foreign language like French were advantages too.

They didn't. None of the people who advertised said they wanted to work for a large family. But there were certainly many people looking for jobs.

An Indian man is looking for a job as a footman. He has worked for seven-and-a-half years for his previous master.

The experienced Indians knew that it was necessary to mention the time spent with a previous master. Spending several years serving one person was seen in a positive light.

'But he doesn't really say what he can do,' Mrs Neville objected.

'Here's one that tells us what he can do,' her daughter said, pushing a newspaper towards her mother.

An Indian man, who can speak English, read and write a little, is looking for a job. Willing to travel.

'We never travel, Martha, and you know it!' Mrs Neville said. 'What if he insists on travelling? We'll have to pack our bags and set out at once, so he's not disappointed.'

Martha giggled and said, 'Here are some ladies looking for jobs, Mother!'

Any lady who is travelling to India and requires a maid, can get in touch. This young Indian woman will serve her well on the ship to India and is willing to serve for three years after too.

***

A young lady, recently come from India, will be happy to accompany any lady back there. She is a good ayah and will be of great help in India too.

For ayahs who came to England, there were often disappointments in store. They were promised a return passage to India or that they would be paid for their return. In both cases, these women were often let down. Some of the ayahs approached the directors of the East India Company for help. Others advertised in the newspaper for a new job. Often, they had to agree to a job that paid nothing, except the ticket back home. When these women reached India, they had nothing to show for the months they had spent away from home and family.

'But they all want to go to India,' Mrs Neville objected. 'And we are not going there.'

'Let's keep looking,' her husband said.

They found more advertisements, one for a lady who could sew and clean well. Another lady said she had served her previous master well, caring for his home and children as if they were her own. 'Now, that's the kind of person I want,' Mrs Neville said, drawing a circle around the advertisement.

'Listen to this,' Martha said.

> An Indian boy, about 13 years of age, has run away from his master's home. He wears a collar around his neck, with the words 'The Lady Bromfield's black.'

Not all English families treated their servants well. There were some that forced the servants to wear a collar or some other mark that indicated whom they belonged to. When servants ran away from their masters, the latter advertised, seeking their return and offering a reward for anyone who caught the runaway servant. These were called 'hue and cry' advertisements.

'How horrible!' Thomas burst out. 'As if he were a dog!'

The children saw many such notices scattered around the newspaper. There was one from a man looking for an 'East India Tawny Black'. Another was looking for a 'Runaway Bengal Boy,' and yet another for 'Thomas Hornsey, a native of the coast of Malabar' because he had run away too.

'There's no point in looking at these,' Mrs Neville said. 'We must look for someone who suits us and whom we will suit.'

'I've found one,' Thomas announced.

> A servant boy, a native of Bengal, called HYDER has left the services of Mrs Ramus. He is 14 years old, tall and thin, and speaks a little English. If Hyder comes back and behaves himself in the future, Mrs Ramus will say nothing.

'Thomas, you silly boy,' his sister said. 'That's a runaway servant.'

'I know,' her brother nodded.

'Do you want to find him and claim the reward?' Mr Neville wanted to know.

'I want to find him, this Hyder, and keep him with us,' Thomas said. 'And that boy with the collar around his neck. And I want to break the collar, so he can be free!'

'I do too!' his sister said and Mr Neville nodded. They sat in silence, thinking of humans who were treated like animals and had to run away to save their lives. And it seemed to them that perhaps they didn't really need someone to serve them that badly.

The newspapers were put away. The Neville family was in no mood to look for help just then.

ACKNOWLEDGEMENTS

It is one thing to dream of writing about ayahs and lascars, the earliest travellers from India to England, and a very different thing to actually write the book. Various people, known and unknown, made this book possible and I am glad of an opportunity to thank them.

I am grateful to the long-ago travellers whose detailed accounts of life in India have helped bring the past gloriously alive for me. They gave me the much-needed cultural context and helped provide relevant background details. Studies by contemporary authors provided valuable insights into the lives of these early travellers and also led me on to other book titles.

My thanks to Vatsala Kaul Banerjee of Hachette India, for her enthusiastic response to the project.

Many thanks to the illustrator of this book, Damini Gupta, for her gorgeous illustrations.

Pramod, my sounding board, my first reader, my go-to person for doubts big and small, is endlessly encouraging. Thank you, your support and faith mean more than I can say.

Aai and Baba, for their constant encouragement, thank you.

Daddy and Mummy, for their affectionate interest in my projects, thank you.

Kavita, for listening to my discussions of my work in progress, and for her unflagging enthusiasm, thank you.

Richa, for being my ready solver of all kinds of issues – moral, ethical, technological – thank you!

The unnamed ayahs and lascars, who left home in search of better opportunities, your stories are endlessly inspiring.

And for Pranav – who fills me with hope of a better world.

SELECT BIBLIOGRAPHY

Compton, Herbert. Ed. *A Master Mariner: Being the Life and Adventures of Captain Robert William Eastwick*. London: T. Fisher Unwin, 1891.

Fay, Eliza. *The Original Letters from India*. Calcutta: Thacker, Spink & Co., 1908.

Fisher, Michael. *Counterflows to Colonialism: Indian Travellers and Settlers in Britain 1600–1857*. Delhi: Permanent Black, 2004.

Hickey, William. *Memoirs*. Edited by Alfred Spence. London: Hurst & Blackett Ltd.

Hill, Charles. *List of Europeans and Others in the English Factories in Bengal at the Time of the Siege of Calcutta in the year 1756*. Calcutta: Office of the Superintendent of Government Printing, India, 1902.

Hunter, William. *An Essay on the Diseases Incident to Indian Seamen, or Lascars, on Long Voyages*. Calcutta: The Honourable Company Press, 1804.

Jaffer, Aaron. *Lascars and Indian Ocean Seafaring 1780-1860: Shipboard Life, Unrest and Mutiny*. Woodbridge: The Boydell Press, 2015.

Visram, Rozina. *Asians in Britain: 400 years of History*. London and Sterling: Pluto Press, 2002.

Visram, Rozina. *Ayahs, Lascars and Princes: The Story of Indians in Britain 1700-1947*. 1986. New York: Routledge, 2015.

https://www.oldbaileyonline.org/browse.jsp?id=t18500610-1040&div=t18500610-1040&terms=Smith_theft_case#highlight. Accessed on 15 May 2023.

IMAGE COPYRIGHT INFORMATION

Page 14, top: *Elizabeth, Sarah and Edward, the Children of Edward Holden Cruttenden;* circa 1763; oil on canvas; artist: Joshua Reynolds; from collection of São Paulo Museum of Art; Wikimedia Commons Public Domain; **bottom left:** Tysoe Hancock and His Family with an Indian Maid_WGA19338, Wikimedia Commons, Public Domain; **bottom right:** Joshua Reynolds self-portrait; B2002.11: Yale Center for British Art; source: mAGNh4nTKTlV5Q – Google Arts & Culture; Wikimedia Public Domain; **Page 24:** An Indian Ayah with two children; Source: http://www.oldindianphotos.in/2011_10_09_archive.html; Wikimedia Commons Public Domain; **Page 25, top:** Lady with Ayah; 1860s; unknown author; source: http://www.columbia.edu/itc/mealac/pritchett/00routesdata/1800_1899/women/tasks/tasks.html; Wikimedia Public Domain; **bottom left:** Title page and frontispiece to Mrs Hannah Glasse's Cookery Book c. 1777; Source: Scan by this contributor from c.1770 original in own possession; Author/Scan: Contributor. Original: W.Wangford c.1777; Wikimedia Commons Public Domain; **bottom right:** Hannah Glasse's recipe for Curry, 1748 - the first known recipe for curry in the English language; Wikimedia Commons Public Domain; **Page 55, top:** Front entrance of the Ayahs' Home; *London City Mission* magazine in 1900; **bottom:** Ayahs' Home, Hackney; 1901; Source: http://www.bl.uk/learning/timeline/external/1900ayahhometl.jpg; Author: Unknown author; held by British Library, UK; Wikimedia Commons Public Domain; Unknown author; Wikimedia Commons Public Domain; **Page 65:** *East Indiaman in a Gale* by Charles Brooking; circa 1759;

oil on canvas; BHC1029: held by Royal Museums Greenwich, UK; Source: National Maritime Museum, Greenwich; Wikimedia Commons Public Domain; **Page 91:** Reproduction ID: P85233; Maker: Marine Photo Service; 1930–39; Materials: Cellulose acetate negative; Source: Three Lascars of the 'Viceroy of India', standing behind the wheel of one of the ship's tenders; Uploaded by NotFromUtrecht; Author: National Maritime Museum from Greenwich, United Kingdom; Wikimedia Commons; **Page 92:** East_Indiamen_Madagascar; circa 1837; Source: National Maritime Museum Greenwich, London; Author: Thomas Goldsworth Dutton; Wikimedia Commons Public Domain; **Page 135, inset:** 1794 Frontispiece of *Dean Mahomet's Travels*; Source: UC Press E-Books Collection: https://publishing.cdlib.org/ucpressebooks/view?docId=ft4h4nb20n&chunk.id=ch2&toc.depth=1&toc.id=ch2&brand=eschol; 1982-2004; Wikimedia Commons Public Domain; **bottom:** Mahomed's Baths: A view of the business premises, in Brighton, of Sake Dean Mahomed; 1826; Image taken from Shampooing; or, benefits resulting from the use of the Indian Vapour Bath as introduced by S.D.M. Second edition; Originally published/produced in Brighton: Creasy & Baker, 1826; Held and digitised by the British Library, ; Wikimedia Commons: Creative Commons CC0 1.0 Universal Public Domain Dedication